*"Many years ago the great British explorer George Mallory,
who was to die on Mount Everest, was asked why did he want to climb it.
He said, 'Because it is there.'*

*Well, space is there, and we're going to climb it,
and the Moon and the planets are there,
and new hopes for knowledge and peace are there.
And, therefore, as we set sail we ask God's blessing
on the most hazardous and dangerous and greatest adventure
on which Man has ever embarked."*

President John F. Kennedy
Rice Stadium September 12, 1962

For my daughter Eve Riley,
may she live to see us stand once more upon the Moon.

CR

For my godsons
Tom & George
and for Shoog, for showing a little boy
that not every star in the night sky was static.

MI

First printed JULY 2019

HARBOUR MOON PUBLISHING
www.harbourmoonpublishing.com

First published in Great Britain 2019

British Library Cataloguing in Publication Data
A catalogue record for this book is available from the British Library
 ISBN - 978-1-9160625-0-4
Printed in the UK

WHERE ONCE WE STOOD

CHRISTOPHER RILEY & MARTIN IMPEY

THE DREAM

Between July 1969 and December 1972, twelve men from Earth landed their spaceships on the Moon. They spent a total of just over 300 hours living and working there, travelling over 100 kilometres across its ancient surface in search of some of the oldest rocks in the solar system. It had taken the combined efforts of the whole American nation to get them there.

The president, John F. Kennedy, who'd first proposed this endeavour, knew it would be hard. In the speech he gave, quoted on the first page of this book, John said he wanted to do it because it would be hard – because when you try and do hard things you learn more. But he could never have imagined just how hard it would be.

What makes sending people to the Moon so difficult is that humans have evolved to breathe, on a planet with an atmosphere. Earth's magnetic field further shields us from the dangerous particles that pour out from the Sun and other stars in our galaxy. But the Moon has none of these defences. Out there, unprotected, you'd die within minutes.

Keeping astronauts alive on a voyage to the Moon demanded a machine that could do all the amazing things our planet does to keep us alive. The resulting spacecraft would also require rocket motors to propel them away from Earth and navigational instruments to help them find their way. It would need room for experiments, tools, rock collection boxes and the paraphernalia of human life – toothbrushes, food parcels, family photos and other mementos to remind them of home.

Transporting three astronauts and all this gear to the Moon and back would need a giant rocket capable of accelerating them to speeds of 11 kilometres per second to leave Earth behind and start falling towards the Moon! To land there safely, they'd need another rocket engine to slow them down to the speed of a gentle jog. Then they'd need a space suit, with all their life support equipment built into it, to protect them outside the spacecraft. After exploring, they'd need one more rocket to launch themselves back off the Moon and break free from its gravity, to fall back to Earth.

There would be millions of problems to solve to make all this possible, and it would take hundreds of thousands of men and women to accomplish it. Only three people would actually fly on each mission, and only two of them would land and walk on the Moon. Six successful landings were made. The twelve people who reached the Moon returned with stories, pictures and silent movies of their experiences; but nothing that would ever truly do justice to what it had meant to them to stand on another world and look back at Earth.

From the sight of a bright morning Sun shining out of an inky black sky, to the delights of playing in the pristine undisturbed dust and airless vacuum of an un-Earthly low gravity landscape, it was hard to convey the human experience of being on another world. But their joy and delight at this experience is evident in the conversations they had on the Moon, as they rediscovered a childlike wonder at what it is to be alive.

This is their story, told through the words they spoke, from a world where once they stood.

The six places on the Moon
where the following stories take place

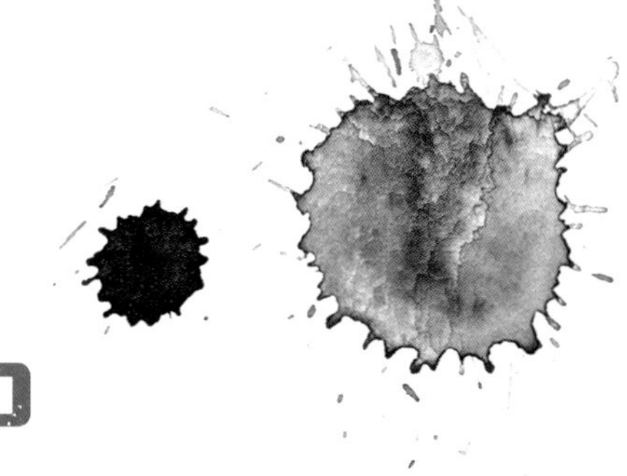

WHERE ONCE WE STOOD

Note on the Book

The Apollo astronauts mixed imperial and metric measurements during their conversations from the Moon, and so we have used whichever units they spoke, and metric when reporting what they were doing. The times and dates we use are based on the time it was in Greenwich, England – from where Universal Time is measured. This means the dates we quote for events on the Moon may not always be the same as those in American history books.
Finally the word “Man” was used in the 1960s and 70s to mean “Mankind”. Today we would say “Humankind”. We have left these words as they were spoken at the time, but the word “Man” with a capital “M” really means men and women. And although no women appear in this book, they played many vital roles in the huge team that put twelve grateful men on the Moon and returned them safely to the Earth.

CDR = Commander

LMP = Lunar Module Pilot

CMP = Command Module Pilot

● = Location of the Lunar Excursion Module or LEM

Chapter 01 - Sea of Tranquility

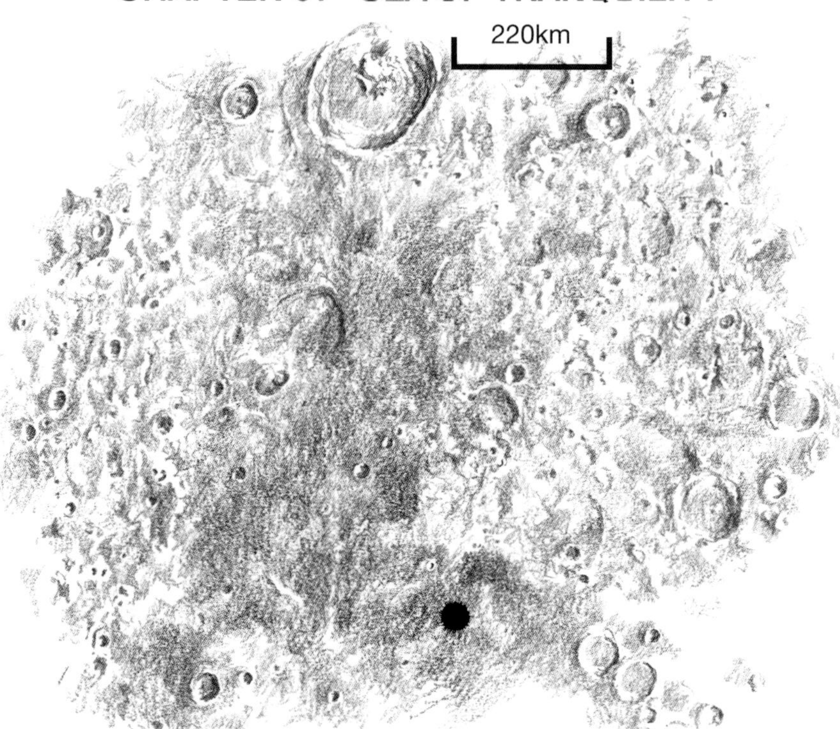

Apollo 11
Neil Armstrong CDR   Buzz Aldrin LMP
Mike Collins CMP

Chapter 02 - The Ocean of Storms

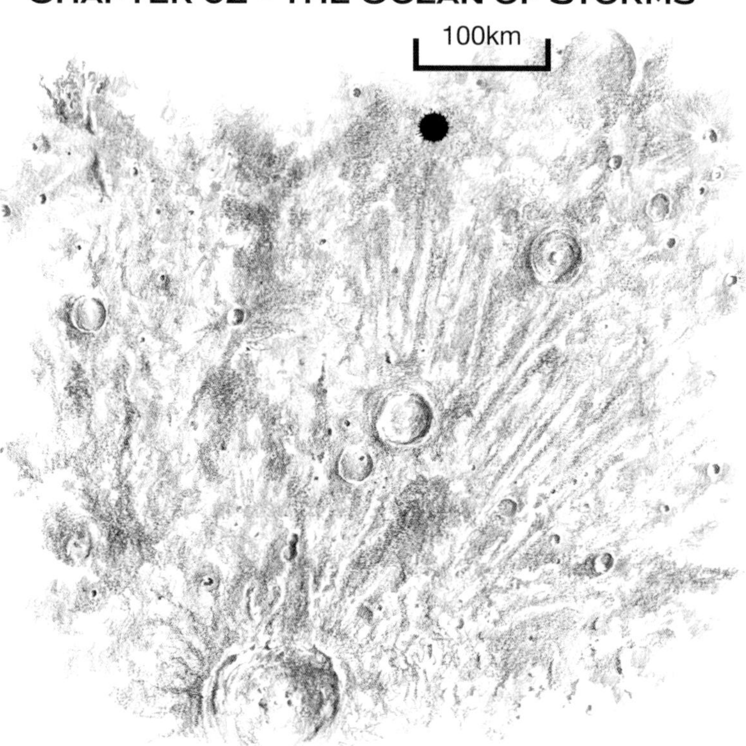

Apollo 12
Pete Conrad CDR   Al Bean LMP
Dick Gordon CMP

Chapter 03 - Fra Mauro Formation

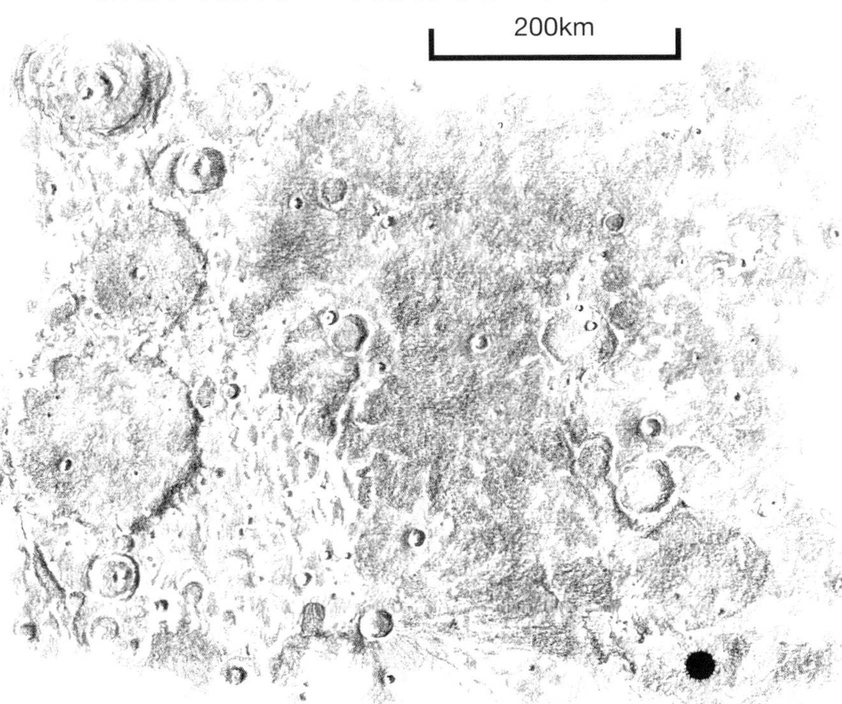

Apollo 14
Al Shepard CDR Ed Mitchell LMP
Stu Roosa CMP

Chapter 04 - Hadley Rille

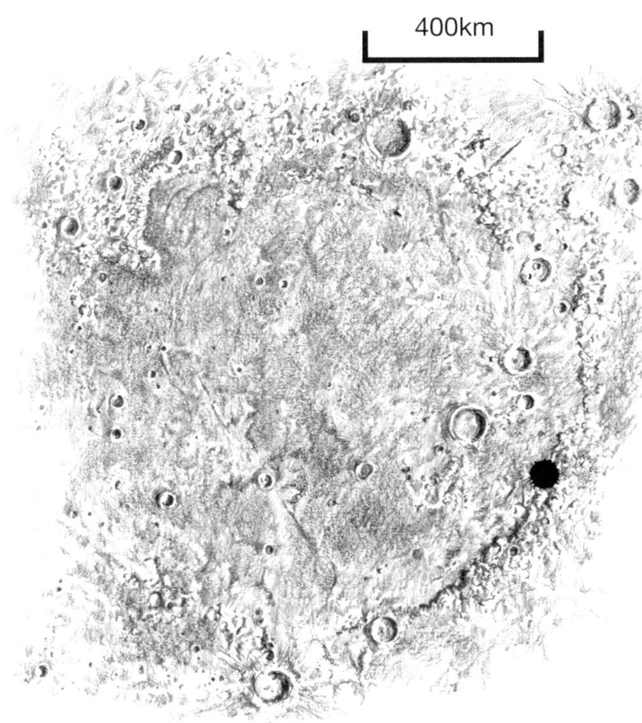

Apollo 15
Dave Scott CDR Jim Irwin LMP
Al Worden CMP

Chapter 05 - Descartes Highlands

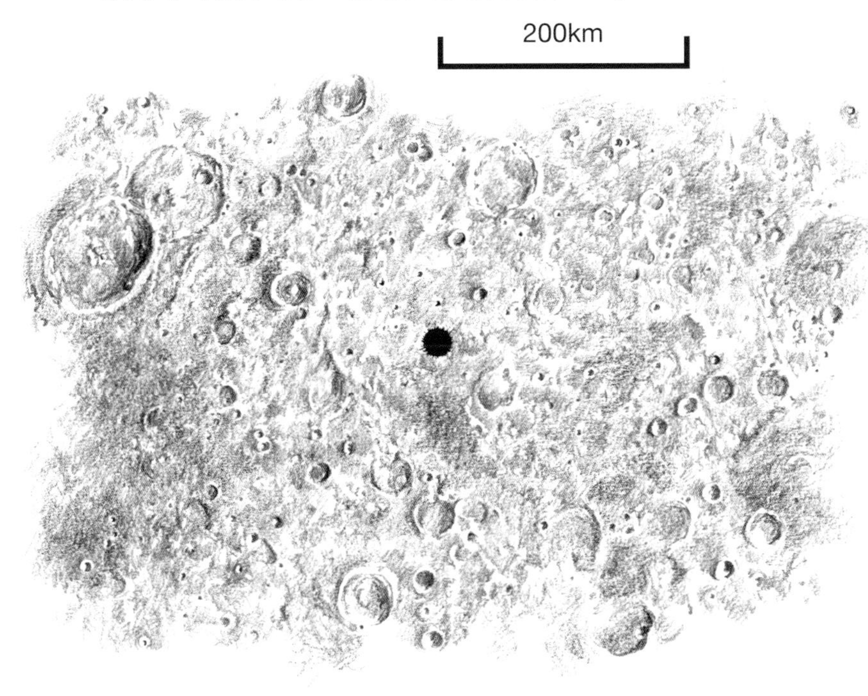

Apollo 16
John Young CDR Charlie Duke LMP
Ken Mattingly CMP

Chapter 06 - The Taurus-Littrow Valley

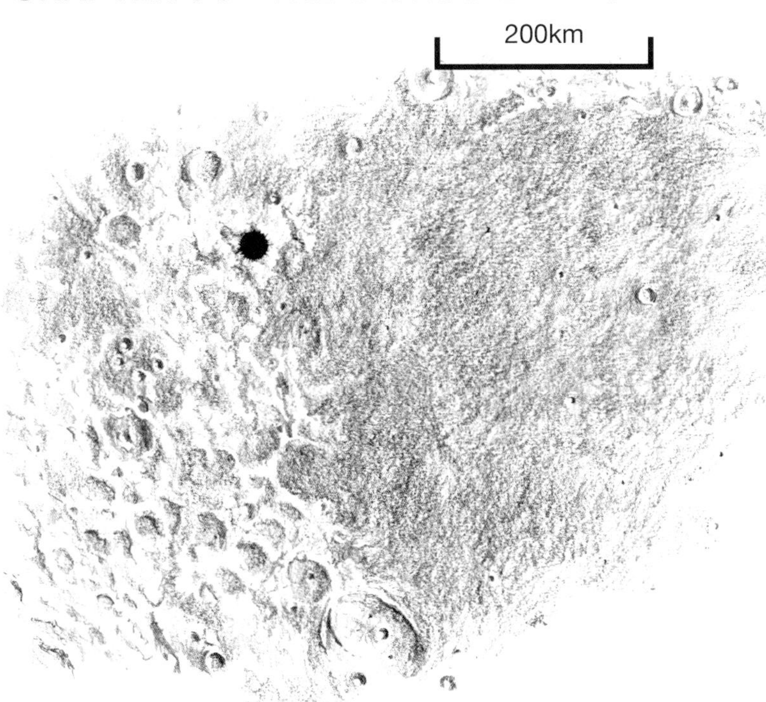

Apollo 17
Gene Cernan CDR Jack Schmitt LMP
Ron Evans CMP

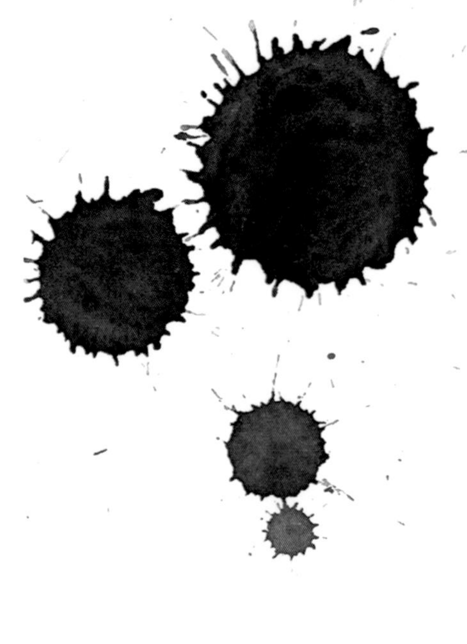

THE SEA OF TRANQUILITY
MONDAY JULY 21ST 1969

ON THE SURFACE OF THE MOON

NEIL ARMSTRONG CDR
(COMMANDER)
BUZZ ALDRIN LMP
(LUNAR MODULE PILOT)

VOICE FROM EARTH

BRUCE MCCANDLESS CAPCOM
(CAPSULE COMMUNICATOR)

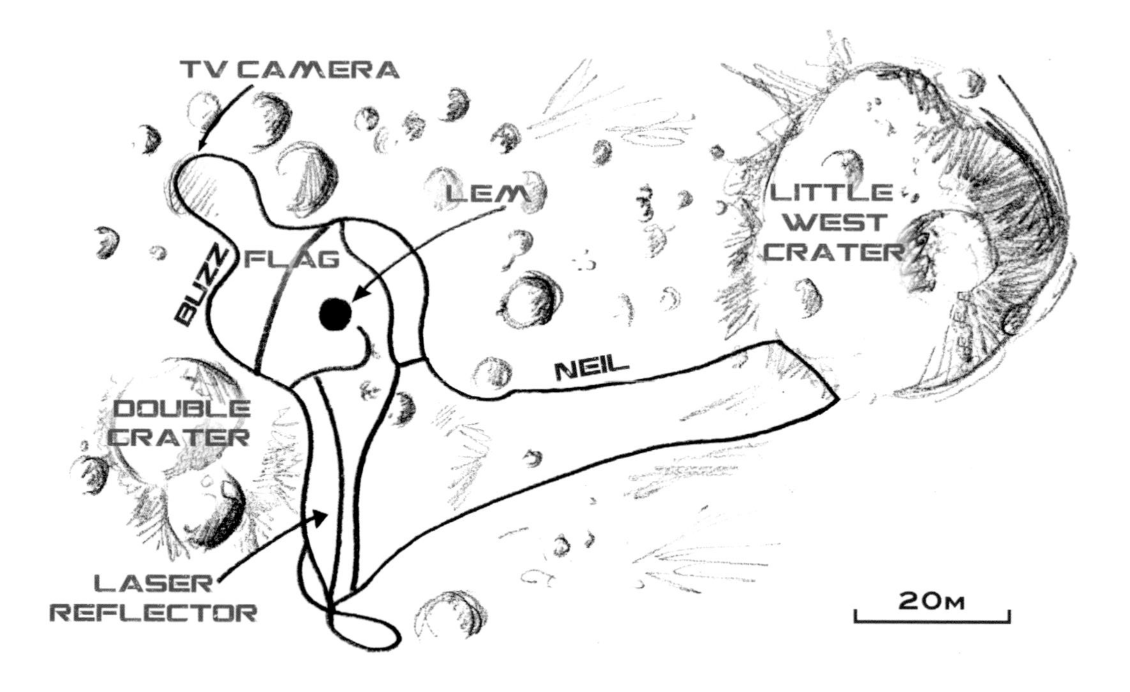

APOLLO 11 LANDING SITE MAP

Part 1
2:40am

"OK. Now comes the gymnastics," says Neil.

"What?" asks Buzz.

"Now comes the gymnastics," Neil repeats.

"Oh, I think it'll be a lot easier," replies Buzz reassuringly.

Neil is on his hands and knees. The weight of his large backpack presses down on him, although with much less weight than it would have done on Earth. Confined inside his spacesuit, all he can see is the floor of the spaceship – called *Eagle* – that's brought him here.

Blindly backing out of a narrow doorway, bum first, with his life support systems strapped to his back, is an undignified way to make his entrance on to the world stage. He feels more like a struggling tortoise than an astronaut about to make history.

Neil is grateful that, at this point, no one except his colleague Buzz can see him.

But all that is about to change. Neil knows he's only minutes away from making an appearance on what is already the most watched live TV broadcast in history. He doesn't like this thought. It makes him anxious. Neil is a quiet, thoughtful man. He dislikes attention. He tries to forget it, concentrating instead on exiting the spaceship.

"Little bit toward me," says Buzz trying to help him. "Straight down. To your left a little bit."

Even though the two men are close enough to touch each other, neither can hear the other one directly. The spaceship door is open and, with no air inside to carry the sound, all is quiet. Instead, the words travel through a microphone inside Buzz's helmet, out of a radio antenna on his backpack, across to Neil's antenna and up to the headphones inside his helmet.

"OK, you're lined up nicely," continues Buzz. "Toward me a little bit, down. OK. Now you're clear."

"OK. Houston, I'm on the porch," says Neil. All this wriggling, inside his bulky pressurised suit, has pushed his heart rate up to 130 beats a minute. He can feel it pumping inside his chest.

Now he's out of the door with his boots on the upper rungs of a short ladder, Neil's next task is to pull a D-shaped handle with his left hand. It triggers a small platform to swing out from the base of the spacecraft beneath him. Fixed to it is a small black and white camera, which Buzz switches on to start transmitting pictures of the bottom of the ladder below Neil's feet.

Two and a half seconds later the signal reaches Earth – and is relayed to hundreds of millions of TV screens across the world.

"OK. We can see you coming down the ladder now," says a voice in Neil's ear. It's a man called Bruce McCandless who's sitting in a hushed room back on Earth, over 400,000 kilometres away. Bruce is surrounded by a bunch of colleagues and friends who have gathered in a large building in the town of Houston, America to offer advice to Neil and Buzz if they get into any trouble.

Neil carries on down the ladder – perhaps aware that more than a billion people are watching him. His concern now is whether he'll sink into the dust when he steps off the ladder. Their spacecraft, known as the Lunar Excursion Module – or "LEM", has legs with big pads on the ends of them to stop them sinking, but Neil has nothing like that on his feet. No one is sure how deep the dust might be on the ground he's about to step on to. No one has ever walked on the Moon before.

In case the dust does swallow him like quicksand, Neil wears a tether so that Buzz can pull him out again if necessary. The tether is also there in case he can't climb back up to the ladder without help.

Neil reaches the last rung and drops off it on to the big round spacecraft footpad below. But instead of stepping straight off on to the Moon, he immediately jumps back up to the first rung, to test how easily he can climb back. Neil is a meticulous planner. Devoted to detail, he thinks everything through before he acts. It's what's helped to keep him alive during a very dangerous career as a test pilot of very fast jets and rocket planes. It's also why he's been chosen to command this first historic flight to land on the surface of another world.

Here on the Moon, Neil finds he can leap the metre back up on to the ladder with just one little push of his legs. Weighing only one sixth of his adult weight, the same as a toddler on Earth, makes him feel like a child again.

"Takes a pretty good little jump…" he reports, his voice edged with excitement.

Neil leans forward a little, craning his neck to see the ground beneath him, checking how much the spacecraft's landing pads have sunk. Trained to relay as much detail as possible back to Earth, and perhaps to take his mind off the enormous number of people now watching, he begins describing what he can see.

"I'm at the foot of the ladder," he says. "The LEM footpads are only depressed in the surface about one or two inches, although the surface appears to be very, very fine-grained as you get close to it. It's almost like a powder."

On Earth, perhaps half of the entire population, which stands at three billion people at this time, have become silent. They hang on Neil's every word. Among the audience are over 400,000 men and women from across America who have devoted most of the last decade of their working lives to the event that is about to happen.

Neil speaks again.
"OK. I'm going to step off the LEM now."

Five seconds of silence follow as Neil composes himself – perhaps silently rehearsing the line he's about to say or marking the moment with a little prayer for everything that's made his next step possible.

Then Neil cautiously lifts his left foot off the spacecraft's pad and places it firmly on to the ground. It's the first footstep any human being has ever taken on a place that isn't Earth.

He leans gingerly into the step – testing the strength of the Moon's surface beneath his boot. Being a man who plans for everything, Neil's come prepared for this moment with a line to mark the occasion. He speaks it.

"That's one small step for a man.
One giant leap for Mankind."

His words so perfectly capture everything about the moment that they are immediately repeated by TV commentators around the world in a hundred different languages. Hanging on these words, the global audience stares at their screens, transfixed at these first live pictures of a man on the Moon.

Some go outside and look up at the Moon themselves – as if to try and glimpse Neil. It suddenly feels like a different Moon to the one they saw yesterday.

Somehow everything about who we are as a species has changed in this moment – and yet, at the same time, nothing has changed.

The clocks tick on.

On a different world, 400,000 kilometres above their heads, Neil continues to revel in the moment; enjoying the privilege of being the only man to ever stand on the Moon.

Curious about just what his boot is doing to the extra-terrestrial ground, he drops his right hand lower on the ladder and steps backwards with his right foot on to the surface – standing for the first time with both feet on the Moon. He's still in the shadow of the spaceship but there's enough sunlight bouncing around the surface to see clearly.

Neil cranes his neck again to see the ground and examines how his left boot has disturbed the dust. Its fine powder sticks to the sole and sides of his boots. He describes it to those listening around the world as being like powdered charcoal; adding an observation about how he only sinks in an inch or so.

The treads of his boots make pleasingly perfect footprints in the flour-fine lunar dust. Like a child walking on fresh snow, Neil marvels for a moment at the first human marks he's leaving here. The surface he's walking on has lain here largely undisturbed since before humans existed.

"I can see the footprints of my boots and the treads in the fine, sandy particles," he says, sounding relieved that he's not sunk any deeper so far.

Eager to let Neil know that he can still be heard back on Earth, Bruce replies, "Neil, this is Houston. We're copying."

Still anxious about pockets of deeper dust, Neil lets go of the ladder. He does a few knee bends to test his balance and then backs cautiously away from the spacecraft.

The alien gravity that he's now walking in for the first time is strangely familiar to him. Both he and Buzz have practised for hours on Earth, walking in simulations of this weaker gravity field which is just one sixth of that on Earth. The teams that trained them have left nothing to chance.

"It's absolutely no trouble to walk around," Neil reports.

Still within the shadow of the spacecraft, he takes the opportunity to study the ground directly beneath the spaceship. The blast from its rocket exhaust has cleaned the dust from the surface leaving scorch marks, but it hasn't left a crater. It reminds him of the landing, when he'd glanced out of the window and been mesmerised by the sight of the dust rushing away over the horizon. With no atmosphere here on the Moon, there is nothing to stop it. Yet as soon as he'd shut down the engine, all the flying dust had immediately dropped to the ground. He'd known this would happen of course. Without any air, there is nothing to hold the dust in a cloud. Knowing this was one thing, but actually seeing it out of the window fascinated him.

"We're essentially on a very level place here," he reports.

As the Earth turns on its axis – 400,000 kilometres above him – the Moon sets on America, simultaneously rising over Australia.

Bruce's team in Houston switches to a new receiving dish in the Australian Outback to continue talking to their faraway friends.

Neil now uses his tether as a pulley system leading back up through the hatch and into the spacecraft. Buzz attaches a bulky photographic camera to the line and Neil gently pulls it down towards him. He backs out into the sunlight to get a better view, being careful not to look directly into the Sun. Here on the Moon, unfiltered by any atmosphere, the Sun's rays are very strong and dangerous.

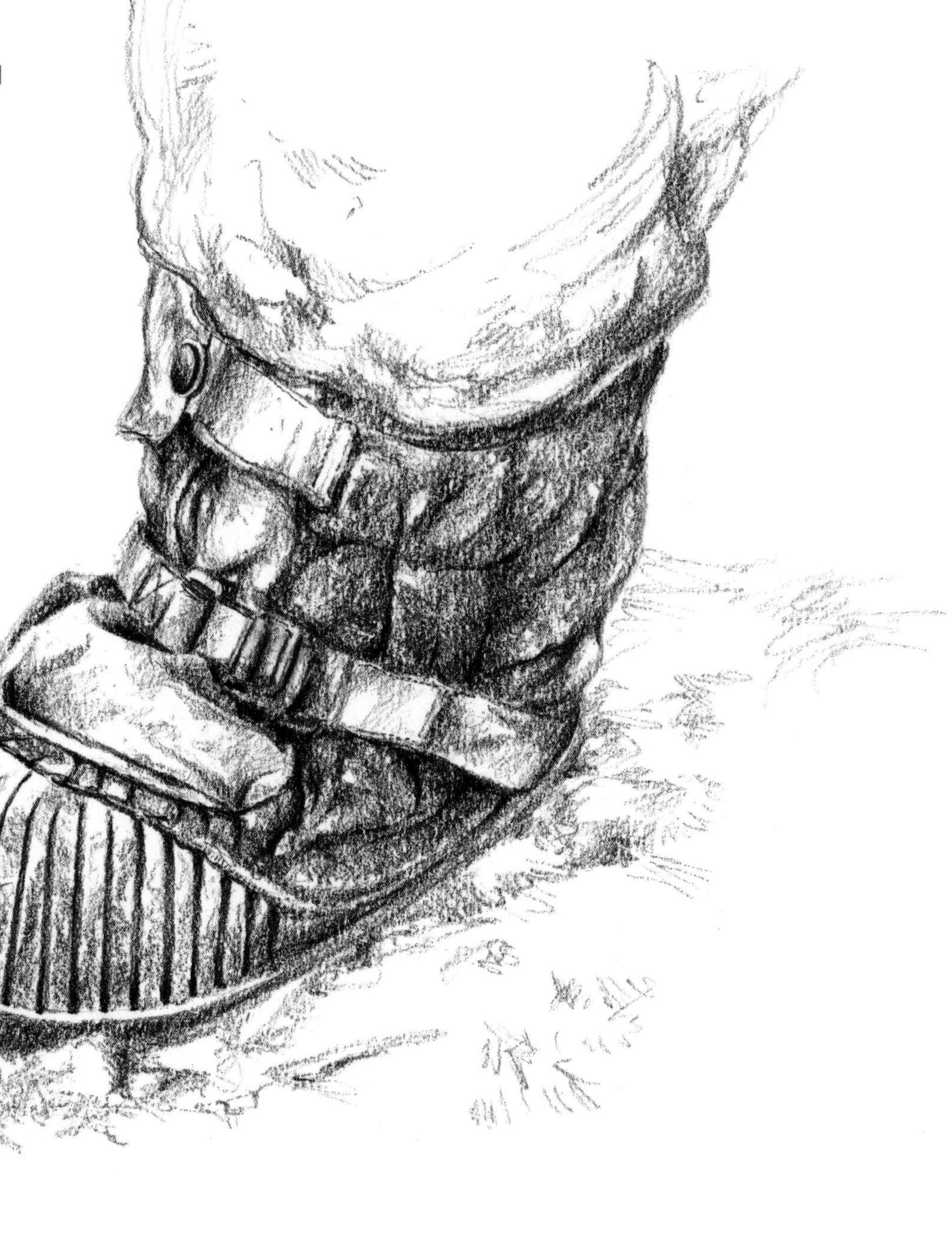

To protect his face from these rays, Neil's outer visor is covered in a thin layer of gold that's just an atom thick. It makes the Moon look slightly green.

Neil steps once more into the shadow of the spacecraft, raising his golden visor to get a clearer view of Buzz through the window, as the camera makes its way down towards him.

This is not a digital camera like those we use today, with a screen to check the pictures on. It has a roll of film inside it, and Neil cannot be sure if the pictures he takes will come out. To make things harder for him, the large pressurised helmet he's wearing means that he is unable to hold the camera up to his face to look through a viewfinder. Instead, Neil mounts it on a bracket on his chest and concentrates on setting the exposure correctly for the bright sunlight and dark shadow of the spacecraft he's still standing behind.

He carefully presses the shutter release switch on the right side. Such a fine movement of his fingers is not easy inside the bulky pressure gloves he's wearing, but he's practised this over and over again and feels confident. Neil feels the shutter inside click satisfyingly.

The photograph, later numbered rather boringly AS11-40-5850, would not win any awards, but it is nonetheless the first photograph ever taken by a human being on another world.

It captures part of the golden foil-covered leg of his spacecraft glowing in the sunlight and the edge of the spaceship, where the words *UNITED STATES* are painted. Beneath it is a large white bag, which Neil discarded before coming down the ladder. It contains empty food bags and other things they no longer need. Stretching out to the horizon, the grey lunar terrain shimmers in the strong morning sunlight* – its smooth, undulating rocky surface like the waves of a sea frozen in time. It feels apt that this place is called the Sea of Tranquility.

Neil turns carefully to his right – taking nine further pictures as he rotates on the spot – until he's back where he started. Together they make up a panorama which reveals the landing site in all its otherworldly glory.

The sunlight bounces strongly around the landscape. Neil and Buzz have arrived in the middle of a lunar morning, yet the black sky fools many of those who will see the photographs in the years that follow into thinking it's night-time. Those people wonder why no stars can be seen in this black sky.

* A lunar day lasts a bit more than 29 Earth days – or about 708 Earth hours. That is to say that the Moon turns just once on its axis with respect to the Sun for every 29 times that the Earth turns on its axis. During that long lunar day the Sun rises slowly over the Moon for about 7 Earth days to reach the lunar midday and then takes another 7 Earth days to go down. It's then dark for around 14 Earth days. To avoid the landing sites getting too hot for the astronauts, all the Apollo missions tried to land during the lunar mornings before the long Moon day had got too hot.

Starlight of course is much fainter than sunlight – which is why stars are no more visible on the Moon during the daytime than they are on Earth, even though the daytime sky on the Moon is black!

It's hard to get used to seeing the Sun in the black sky. Neil has seen it before, when he's previously been above the Earth's atmosphere on experimental rocket plane flights, as well as during a brief space flight called Gemini 8. But this is the first time he's stood in a landscape and seen the Sun in a black sky. It feels odd. The sunlight out here is so strong that it makes the relatively dark lunar surface, which Neil knows to be as dark as the tarmac on a road, seem very bright indeed. It appears so bright that he has to shut the lens of his camera right down to make sure the pictures come out.

With his first photos snapped, Neil turns his attention to collecting the first moon rocks to bring back to Earth. The team call this the "contingency sample" – a contingency that ensures they will at least have a small sample of moon rock to study back on Earth should Neil and Buzz suddenly have to leave the Moon in a hurry.

Bending over or kneeling down, to pick up this contingency sample with his hands, is impossible inside his awkward pressurised space suit. So instead Neil carries a tool with a long collapsible arm, which he can use to pick up rocks and dirt.

The rods in the arm are all connected by an elasticated cord, which snaps them together like the poles of a small tent. Neil quickly puts it together and then teases out a cylindrical cloth scoop at one end, which he will use to scoop up a sample. Buzz watches with interest from the window as Neil attempts to collect something with it.

"Looks like it's a little difficult to dig through the initial crust..." Buzz remarks.

"This is very interesting," says Neil, still fascinated by every bit of his extraterrestrial encounter. "It's a very soft surface, but here and there I run into a very hard surface."
He takes aim at two rocks to his left. "I'll try to get a rock in here," he announces.

Neil carries on looking for easy pickings – small rocks lying on the surface that he can easily scoop into the cloth cup. His back is to the Sun, and his long shadow is cast ahead of him as he leans to his right, scouring the area for more rocks to grab.

"That looks beautiful from here, Neil," says Buzz, itching to get out there himself.

Neil pauses to look at the terrain around him. "It has a stark beauty all its own," he observes. "It's like much of the high desert of the United States," he adds, recalling areas where he's lived in California's Mojave Desert.
"It's different, but it's very pretty out here."

Neil's attention returns to the detail of the rocks he's trying to collect by his feet. They are known as basalt – which commonly erupts from volcanoes on Earth and cools very quickly before any big crystals can grow. But there's another sort of rock that Neil has noticed. Even through his helmet Neil can see lots of little pits in them, which he describes as looking like the scars he's seen when air gun shot hits rocks on Earth. He's right. These other rocks he's collecting are called breccias, and they are typically made up of lots of bits of other rocks – smashed up by the endless impact of meteorites on the Moon's surface over millions of years.

Still excited by the properties of the lunar dirt, Neil prods and pokes the sampler into the ground, noting that it goes in 6–8 inches, (about 15–20cm). He turns and throws a ring from the sampling tool off to his right. It flies a delightfully long distance in the lower lunar gravity.

"Didn't know you could throw so far!" jokes Buzz, still watching from the window.

Neil laughs in delight. "You can really throw things a long way up here," he smiles.

In total, Neil manages to gather about a kilogram of contingency rock samples and radios to Bruce that the sample is safely stowed.

His 15 minutes alone on the Moon, as the only human being in history ever to have walked here, is almost over. The second man on the Moon is about to arrive.

PART 2
3:03AM

Buzz adjusts the camera that he's been using to film Neil through the window, resetting it to take a single snap every second.
"OK. Are you ready for me to come out?" he asks Neil.
"All set," says Neil, who's positioned himself outside to get a clear view of Buzz as his partner wriggles out of the hatch feet first. There's only just enough room for their life support backpack, known as a PLSS, to clear the doorway.

"OK. Your PLSS looks like it is clearing OK," says Neil. "Your toes are about to come over the sill. OK. Now drop your PLSS down."

Buzz slides clear of the doorway.

"There you go," says Neil, snapping a series of photographs of Buzz's efforts. "You're clear!"
"You need a little bit of arching of the back to come down," reports Buzz.
"How far are my feet from the edge?"
"You're right at the edge of the porch," replies Neil. "Looks good."
"OK. Now I want to back up and partially close the hatch," says Buzz, adding, "making sure not to lock it on my way out."
Neil laughs nervously. "A particularly good thought."

Should even a small amount of air leak back into the spacecraft's cabin from the oxygen supply tanks onboard, while they are outside, the pressure could force the door shut – locking them both outside. Neither astronaut wants to think about that at this time.

"That's our home for the next couple of hours and we want to take good care of it," adds Buzz.

Neil continues to take photographs of Buzz coming down the ladder, for future missions to learn from.
"OK. I'm on the top step and I can look down over the landing gear pads," reports Buzz, switching to a running commentary. "It's a very simple matter to hop down from one step to the next."

"Yes. I found I could be very comfortable, and walking is also very comfortable," replies Neil, delighted at the chance to now compare his experiences with someone else. "You've got three more steps and then a long one," continues Neil.

Buzz drops off the last step on to the footpad.
"There you go," says Neil.
Keen to try getting back up before heading on to the Moon, as Neil had done, Buzz also tries to jump up to the bottom rung. But he doesn't quite make it – dropping gracefully back on to the footpad.
"A little more. About another inch," says Neil, offering advice.
Buzz tries again and lands firmly on the lowest rung.
"There, you've got it," says Neil.

Before continuing, Buzz realises he needs to go to the toilet. Standing still for a moment at the bottom of the ladder, he relaxes his bladder. The urine trickles down a tube and into a bag strapped on his leg inside his suit. Relieved, he drops down to the footpad and looks around. He's glad to be outside the confines of the spacecraft after being cooped up inside it for days.

"Beautiful view!" he declares, somewhat lost for words.
"Isn't that something!" replies Neil. "Magnificent sight out here."
"Magnificent desolation," replies Buzz, playing off Neil's word. "Magnificent desolation," he repeats to himself. It kind of sums it up nicely.

Buzz hops backwards on to the surface to join Neil and turns to inspect the spacecraft and the landing site. The pleasure that Neil felt, in making his first footprints in the fine powdery surface, appeals to Buzz too.
"Very fine powder, isn't it?" says Buzz.
"Isn't it fine?" Neil agrees. "Notice how you can kick it out."

The pair kick the dust around a bit, marvelling at how it moves in the vacuum – flying forwards and then instantly dropping back to the surface.

Keen to experience the freedom of the lower gravity for himself, Buzz moves back from the ladder and tries a few short jumps – bending his knees to launch himself off the ground. Neil tries some too. Like a pair of excited schoolkids they repeatedly leap up high – revelling in the length of time it takes them to come back down. As they go higher, their bulky backpacks start to pull them over and Neil comes close to falling on his back. *That's enough of that*, he decides.

Undeterred, Buzz is still keen to try out the full range of movements that he can do here on the Moon. Grabbing the ladder with his right hand, he flexes his left knee, reaching down to try to touch the ground with his left hand. It's the one thing that their pressurised suits restrict them from doing, but Buzz has a good go and scrapes his knee in the dirt. The lunar dust sticks to his white suit – not because it's wet, but because it's incredibly dry. The stickiness comes from tiny electrical charges between the fine moon dust particles.

Buzz lets go of the ladder again and resumes his experiments in movement. Shifting his weight from foot to foot, he finds that his backpack takes time to catch up with him – which is a bit of a distraction. He hops around some more, reporting that the ground feels slightly slippery when he tries to stop – the fine lunar powder perhaps travelling on a little under his boots.

"I start to lose my balance in one direction," he tells Bruce over the radio, explaining that if he's not careful it can begin to feel like he's a little bit drunk.

Buzz soon realises that he needs to keep an eye out four or five steps ahead. He stops to take in the view again. With no familiar landmarks or features to judge scale, Buzz finds it impossible to appreciate how far away the horizon is. But he can see that it's curved. At just one sixth of the size of his home planet, the curvature of the horizon is pronounced. He and Neil are definitely standing on a sphere!

While Buzz has been reporting back on what it's like to move around on the Moon in one sixth of Earth's gravity, Neil's been busy repositioning the live TV camera so that everyone back home can keep up with their activities. With that task completed, Neil turns his attention to unveiling a commemorative plaque. For the benefit of the audience watching around the world who can't see what's on it, Neil describes the inscription.

"There's two hemispheres of the Earth. Underneath it says, 'Here men from the planet Earth first set foot upon the Moon, July 1969 A.D. We came in peace for all Mankind.' It has the crew members' signatures and the signature of the President of the United States."

With this brief ceremony concluded, the pair of historic explorers return to more mundane matters. The TV camera, which filmed Neil's first step on to the Moon, is still fixed to the fold out platform on the spacecraft and only shows a very tight view of the bottom of the ladder. Neil will now move it further away from the spacecraft and fix it to a stand to give everyone back on Earth a wider view of what they get up to next.

"Would you pull out some cable for me, Buzz?" asks Neil.
"OK," replies Buzz. "How's the temperature look on there?"

On the Moon, with no air to retain the heat from the Sun, it's very cold in the shade – typically 150 degrees Centigrade below zero. But as soon as you step into the sunshine, the heat instantly hits 180 degrees above zero. These dramatic swings of temperature are well known because of the robotic landers that reached the Moon in the years before Neil and Buzz arrived.

But it's still a challenge for the engineers who've designed the equipment they're using, and the spacesuits they're wearing, to keep the mission running.

"Temperature of the camera is showing cold," reports Neil.
"I'm a little cool," replies Buzz. "I think I'll change. I'm on intermediate cooling now."

Running through a network of tiny tubes, stitched into the underwear that they're both wearing, runs a supply of water that can carry their body heat away and also bring them warmth. Each of them can adjust the temperature setting using a lever on their backpacks.

His suit is so good at maintaining a comfortable temperature that, to his surprise, Neil finds he never needs to make a single adjustment. But there's one part of his body the suit can't help to keep cool, and that's his hands. Neil has chosen not to wear inner gloves so that he can feel things more easily through the multiple layers of protective material. But without these extra gloves, his hands are getting hotter than he expected and have become very sweaty – so much so that he's now losing the ability to grip things. To compensate, he has to squeeze his fingers to grip even tighter as he carries the TV camera and stand into position. Neil is just putting it down again when something catches his eye.

"Something interesting in the bottom of this little crater here..." he reports. Neil has spotted a glassy substance in the tiny crater by his feet, caused when a rock struck the Moon at such high speed that it melted the surface.
"Keep going," says Buzz, jolting Neil back to the camera task. "We've got a lot more," Buzz continues, reporting on the remaining length of TV cable still to stretch out.
"How far would you say I am, Buzz?" asks Neil, returning to his task.
"Forty, fifty feet," replies Buzz. "Why don't you turn around and let them get a view from there and see what the field-of-view looks like?" he adds.
"OK. I don't want to go into the Sun if I can avoid it," Neil warns, aware that the camera is very sensitive and its sensors could be damaged if pointed at the Sun.

"I'll just leave it. Tell me if you've got a picture, Houston," Neil requests.

"We've got a beautiful picture, Neil," says Bruce, marvelling at the new view.

Neil proceeds to slowly pan the camera around the site, stopping it every few degrees for Bruce and the others on Earth to enjoy the show.

"We see Buzz going about his work," interrupts Bruce, more in awe at the sight of a person in this alien landscape than the landscape itself.

While Neil has been working on the TV camera, Buzz has been trying to stick a pole topped with a white flag into the ground. The flag is designed to catch millions of tiny particles, smaller than an atom, which stream out from the Sun.

On Earth, these solar particles are deflected by our planet's magnetic field and the atmosphere, never making it to the ground. But here on the Moon, with neither of those protective shields, they constantly crash into the surface, and there's a chance to catch them with the flag. That's if Buzz can get it to stand up! The flag's pole is supposed to push into the ground like a tent peg. But, deeper than 10-12 cm, the Moon's surface is proving too hard. He lets go gingerly and, to his delight, it stays upright.

There's one more flag to put up that's not on their checklist. It's the American flag – an afterthought – but an important, symbolic one for those watching back home who contributed so much to make this moonwalk possible. Without room onboard the spacecraft to carry it, the ingenious engineers have stored it in a protective tube on the left side of the spacecraft's ladder. Neil goes to retrieve it.

Unlike the solar collecting device, this flagpole comes in two halves; a lower section they can push into the ground more easily, and then an upper section that slots into the lower pole, from which the flag will fly. Despite this design, Neil still can't get the lower pole more than 15 cm into the ground. They have to tilt the whole thing backwards to make it stand up.

Of course, without an atmosphere on the Moon, there will be no breeze for the flag to fly. But NASA engineers have thought of that, incorporating a horizontal strut at the top of the pole from which the nylon flag will hang. It's designed to extend outwards when pulled, but it's very stiff. Neil grabs hold of the pole and Buzz tugs at the flag to try and force it.

"That's good. See if you can pull that end off a little bit," says Neil.

"It won't go up," replies Buzz.

Try as they might to fully extend it, the top rod refuses to budge, leaving the flag with a curious ripple. It looks as if the flag is flapping. In fact, it's such a good look that future astronauts will intentionally leave the top rod at this length to create the same "flying flag" effect at their landing sites.

Buzz steps back to admire their work. He feels moved to salute the flag as Neil takes his picture. For a brief moment, he contemplates the hundreds of millions of people back on Earth watching him through the TV camera, standing there by the flag. He feels an almost mystical connection with them.

With their flag proudly flying at the landing site, Neil and Buzz return to their task checklist. It says that Neil is to head back to the spacecraft to collect a metal box to fill with more rocks, while Buzz should do some experiments in how a person can move around on the Moon.

After checking that Bruce can see him in the TV camera, Buzz begins to try out some different ways of walking. First he lollops towards the camera.

"You do have to be rather careful to keep track of where your centre of mass is," he reports. "Sometimes it takes about two or three paces to make sure you've got your feet underneath you."

Buzz turns and heads back towards the spacecraft, attempting to change direction abruptly to see what happens. He seems to have quickly adapted to the gravity and the surface he's on.

"I can change direction like a football player. You just have to put a foot out to the side and cut a little bit," he says.

Buzz turns again and moves back towards the TV camera, now doing a sort of two-footed jump.

"The so-called kangaroo hop does work," he continues, "but it seems as though your forward mobility is not quite as good as one foot after another."

Tiring of the kangaroo jump, Buzz switches back to a more regular two-footed lope.

The 'lunar lope' involves leaving the ground with both feet to take advantage of the lower gravity, and then coming down with one foot in a regular running position. Both Neil and Buzz soon find that this is the most enjoyable way to get around. Neil travels the furthest during their excursion – covering up to 150 metres at a time before resting and taking pictures.

Both men feel the pressure of time slipping away. They long for more, to extend their precious experience here on the Moon. They are already behind on their tasks when Bruce asks them to both come and stand in front of the camera for something very important.

"Neil and Buzz, the President of the United States is in his office now and would like to say a few words to you," says Bruce. "Over."

"That would be an honour," says Neil.

It's almost midnight back on Earth in Washington – the capital city of America, where the latest President, Richard Nixon, is sitting at a large desk in his larger office.

"Hello, Neil and Buzz. I'm talking to you by telephone from the Oval Room at the White House, and this certainly has to be the most historic telephone call ever made. I just can't tell you how proud we all are of what you have done..." The end of Richard's sentence is lost on the way to the Moon, but Neil and Buzz understand what he is trying to say.

Richard continues. "For every American, this has to be the proudest day of our lives. And for people all over the world, I am sure they too, join with Americans in recognising what an immense feat this is." A static crackle of silence breaks into the call.

"Because of what you have done, the heavens have become a part of Man's world. And as you talk to us from the Sea of Tranquility, it inspires us to redouble our efforts to bring peace and tranquility to Earth. For one priceless moment in the whole history of Man, all the people on this Earth are truly one; one in their pride in what you have done, and one in our prayers that you will return safely to Earth."

Neil and Buzz thank Richard for his words and tell him how honoured they are to have been a part of all this. They conclude by saying that they look forward to seeing him when they get back to Earth. With that, the first interplanetary phone call in history is over.

Now even further behind in their tasks, the two astronauts resume their to-do lists. Buzz's next job is to walk around kicking at the lunar dust. His boot sends it spraying out in front of him in a very satisfying way. The camera watching out of the spacecraft window records the trajectories that the dust particles take. Buzz repeats it again and again, in different directions, switching feet for fun. He doesn't seem to tire of the strange arcs the sprays make through the vacuum in the Moon's lower gravity.

Buzz heads back into the shadow of the spacecraft to retrieve the camera for his next task: taking detailed photographs of his boot prints in the lunar dust. After the strong glare of the Sun, it takes his eyes a while to adapt to the relative darkness of the shade again.

Buzz is now hunting for a patch of undisturbed lunar surface, close to the spacecraft, that he can photograph before placing a boot print into it and taking another picture. This task has been requested by researchers back on Earth who want to better understand the lunar surface for future missions. But the photographs Buzz is about to take will become far more useful than that.

The first picture Buzz snaps shows a typical portion of the grey ground. The morning sun is to his right and casts long shadows of each tiny grain of rock or clump of dirt. Then he brings in his right leg and firmly presses the sole of his boot into the soft lunar dirt. He carefully lifts his foot back out of view again and snaps a couple of pictures of the crisp fresh boot print.

The first of these boot print pictures will become one of the most reproduced in history – symbolising the entire human effort needed to get him here. Somehow the footprint speaks to everyone back on Earth – representing the spirit of exploration that has carried our species to the furthest corners of our home planet and now to the surface of another world.

While Buzz is immortalising their moonwalk, Neil is working hard to collect more rock samples to bring back for the geologists. He knows that he needs to get as far away from the spacecraft as possible, to make sure he gets samples that haven't been contaminated by the rocket's engine. But this will mean breaking one of the mission rules, which demands that both astronauts stay within view of the TV camera.

Neil weighs it up and decides the reward is worth the rule breaking. He's spied the rim of a crater out of view of the camera. He thinks the crater might have rocks from deeper below the surface, dug out by the impact that made it. So while everyone is distracted watching Buzz kicking up dust, he rushes off to his furthest location and starts collecting.

Neil makes about 20 round trips to the site, bringing back scoops of dirt and rock that he can drop into the collection box beside the spacecraft. The rocks he collects will be studied for decades, and possibly centuries to come. It's perhaps the most scientifically productive eight minutes of his life.

Neil returns to the shade of the spacecraft with his last sample and is working to squeeze everything he's collected into a box, when he looks up and catches sight of Buzz standing further away. Set against the inky black infinity of space beyond, his pal backlit by sunshine, Neil is immediately struck by the beauty of the view. Guessing the framing, he snaps a single picture. Buzz is a bit small in it so Neil steps forward to take it again.

As he does so, Buzz turns towards Neil and raises his left arm to read the checklist sewn on to his wrist. Neil presses the shutter once again. This photograph, later named AS11-40-5903, is the 33rd photograph he's taken outside the spacecraft that day – but it will attract the most attention.

Although Neil's almost cut the top off Buzz's backpack and helmet, the picture captures a perfect, crisp portrait of a human being standing on the Moon: his bright white spacesuit set against a deep black sky, and the gold visor clearly reflecting Neil and the spacecraft that's brought them both there.

In the decades that follow, this image will become the most reproduced picture of all the Apollo missions. It epitomises everything about human ingenuity and our determination to explore.

Buzz starts to pull out experiments from the bottom of their spacecraft. One of them is a flat surface the size of a small square table. It's covered in over 200 tiny spherical mirrors. Once Neil and Buzz have left, lasers will be bounced off it from Earth to accurately measure the distance to the Moon.

Of course, trying to hit this relatively tiny table top from Earth will not be easy. The people who are going to attempt it liken their task to trying to hit a coin with a rifle bullet from three kilometres away. Not only that, but trying to detect the light which bounces back from it will be even harder.

Of the one hundred quadrillion (that's 10 with 17 zeros – 1000,000,000,000,000,000) packets of light, known as photons, which they aim at the reflector, only one will bounce back to them every few seconds.

But Buzz hasn't time to think about all that right now. With the mirrored instrument in his right hand and another device for listening for moonquakes* in his left, he sets off to find some level ground to set them on.

Within minutes of laying out these experiments, they are up and running. The laser team back on Earth start trying to locate the mirror. It's not easy. They are not entirely sure exactly where Neil and Buzz have landed.

It will take them a few weeks to get a measurement.**

The moonquake team enjoy quicker success, soon picking up the footsteps of the two astronauts. They can even tell when Neil and Buzz are hurrying, as they both race around the landing site trying to squeeze as many jobs as possible into the remaining minutes they have.

Neil is particularly busy – rushing to take photographs of the locations he's sampled rocks from. The TV camera records him running past at an estimated 3.5 kilometres per hour – slower than a brisk walking pace on Earth, but a record-breaking speed for someone on the Moon.

As Neil races around the surface, Buzz is triggering more vibrations by trying to hammer a long, hollow metal tube into the ground. His aim is to collect a cylindrical core of rock from below the surface.

* Like earthquakes, moonquakes are vibrations that rumble through the Moon when parts of its crust shift and move. During each Apollo mission, once the Lunar Excursion Module had returned the astronauts to the mothership in orbit, they would jettison it. Eventually it would crash back on to the Moon. The vibrations from its impact travelling through the Moon would be detected moments later at the landing sites. The timings of the arrival of these vibrations would help us understand what the inside of the Moon might be made of.

** Despite the challenges of bouncing a laser off the mirrors placed on the Moon, they succeeded, recording the average distance from the Earth to the Moon as 385,000.6 kilometres – one of the most accurate distance measurements ever made.

"I hope you're watching how hard I have to hit this into the ground," Buzz says to Bruce. By now he's whacking it so hard that the top of the tube is becoming dented, but it's still only penetrated about the length of his thumb into the Moon's surface. He just can't get it any deeper. He pulls it out and shows it to Neil who confirms that he has indeed managed to sample something.

"You got it! Sampled!" chuckles Neil.

The pair spend their remaining time stowing their samples into the rock box and retrieving the solar wind flag to bring back those precious particles from the Sun. In these final moments on the Moon, both Neil and Buzz are working flat out to get everything ready for their departure. Each of them feels acutely aware of just how rushed they are. With no time for Neil to clean the lunar dirt off his colleague's suit as planned, Buzz heads straight back up the ladder – his precious two hours and eight minutes on the Moon's surface over.

"OK. Adios, amigo," says Buzz, switching to Spanish for his last words on the Moon.

Neil is also too busy to photograph him heading back into the spaceship. Instead he is frantically shovelling moon dust into the remaining sample boxes to cushion the individual rock samples he's gathered. Above him, Buzz pushes the hatch open and wriggles back into the LEM on his belly – his backpack just clearing the doorway.

Back on the surface, Neil realises he's overfilled the sample box with lunar dirt and is now struggling to close the lid. Aware that his flight to the Moon might be the only time humans come this way, Neil is determined to bring back as much lunar material as he can squeeze into the box. It takes all his strength and effort to close and lock it. But now he has to heave the full box a few metres out to make the 'tether line' tight and start hauling it up to Buzz. Thankfully the box only weighs a sixth of what it will on Earth. But it's still hard work, and pushes his heart rate up to 160 beats a minute – over two and a half times the rate when he's resting.

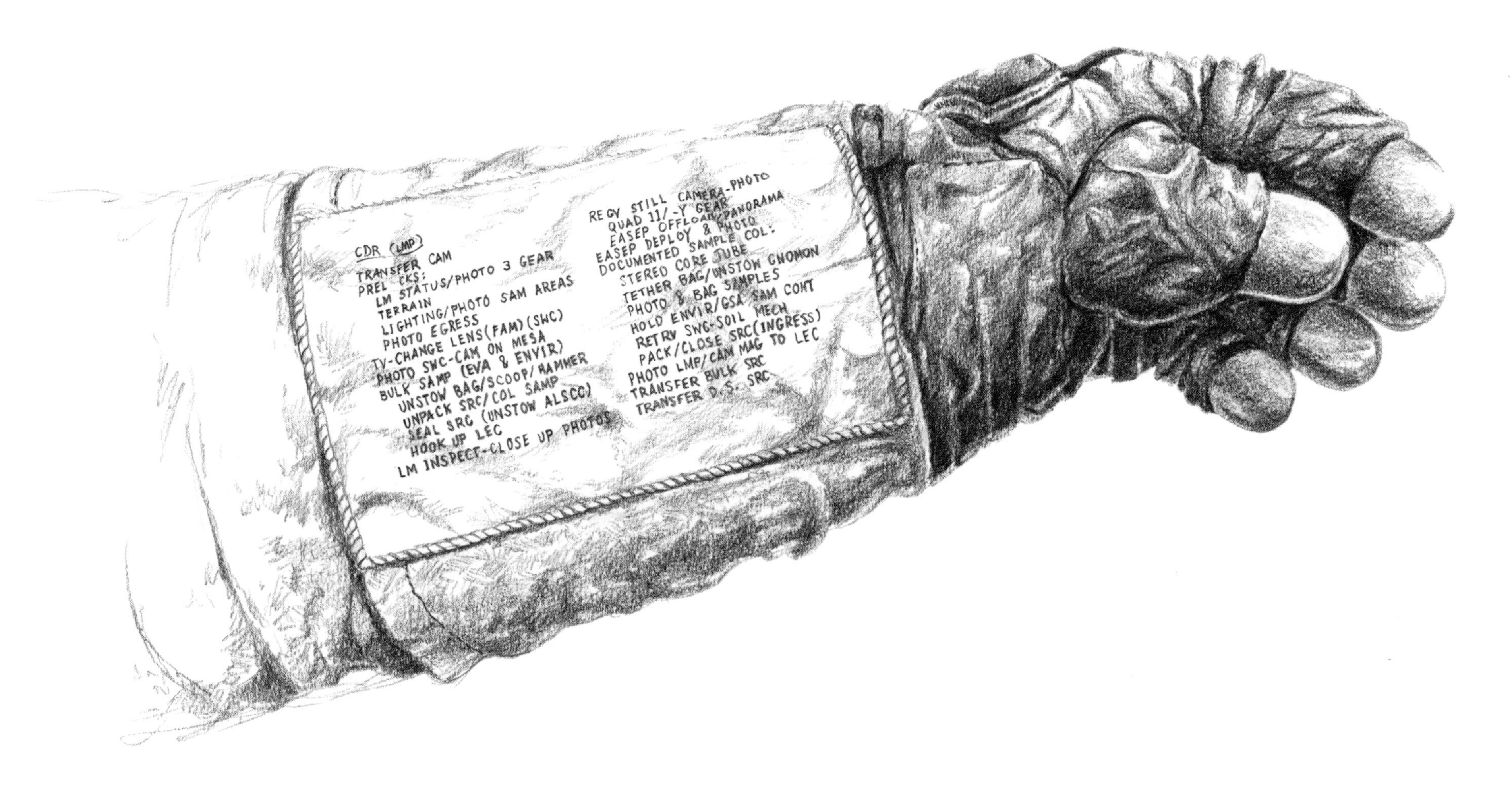

As he pulls on the line, it picks up the fine, powdery moon dust and showers him in it. It makes his job even harder. With one last tug, the box makes it through the hatch. Neil's work here is done.

He's about to step off the Moon for the last time when he remembers something. He stops.
"How about that package out of your sleeve? Get that?" asks Neil, referring to a small packet of personal items which he and Buzz wanted to place on the Moon.
"No!" replies Buzz, annoyed that he's forgotten it.
"Want it now?" he asks.
"Guess so," says Neil.

Buzz reaches into his right shoulder pocket and pulls out the small pouch. He holds it for a moment and then drops it out of the door. It lands on the Moon just to the right of his crewmate. Neil turns and nudges it in the dust with his foot, and then asks Buzz if it looks OK.

"OK," replies Buzz glancing down.

Inside the pouch is a mission patch for Apollo 1, with the names of the three astronauts who were due to fly on it – Gus, Ed and Roger. All three men had died two years earlier in a fire inside their spaceship during a practice on the launch pad. Neil and Buzz pause to remember their friends. Also inside are two medals commemorating Soviet cosmonauts: Yuri – the first man ever to fly in space, who was later killed in a plane crash, and Vladimir – who died when his spacecraft crashed back to Earth after its parachutes failed to open. Although Neil and Buzz never met the two cosmonauts, they feel a bond connecting them.
The sacrifices of all these men are part of the reason Neil and Buzz are on the Moon today.

Remembering them, Neil steps off the Moon – his life forever changed by the time he's spent there, where once he stood.

WHITE
GRISSOM
CHAFFEE
APOLLO 1

The Ocean of Storms
Wednesday November 19th, 1969

On the surface of the moon

Pete Conrad CDR
(Commander)
Al Bean LMP
(Lunar Module Pilot)

Voice from earth

Ed Gibson CAPCOM-1 (Capsule Communicator)
Paul Weitz CAPCOM-2 (Capsule Communicator)

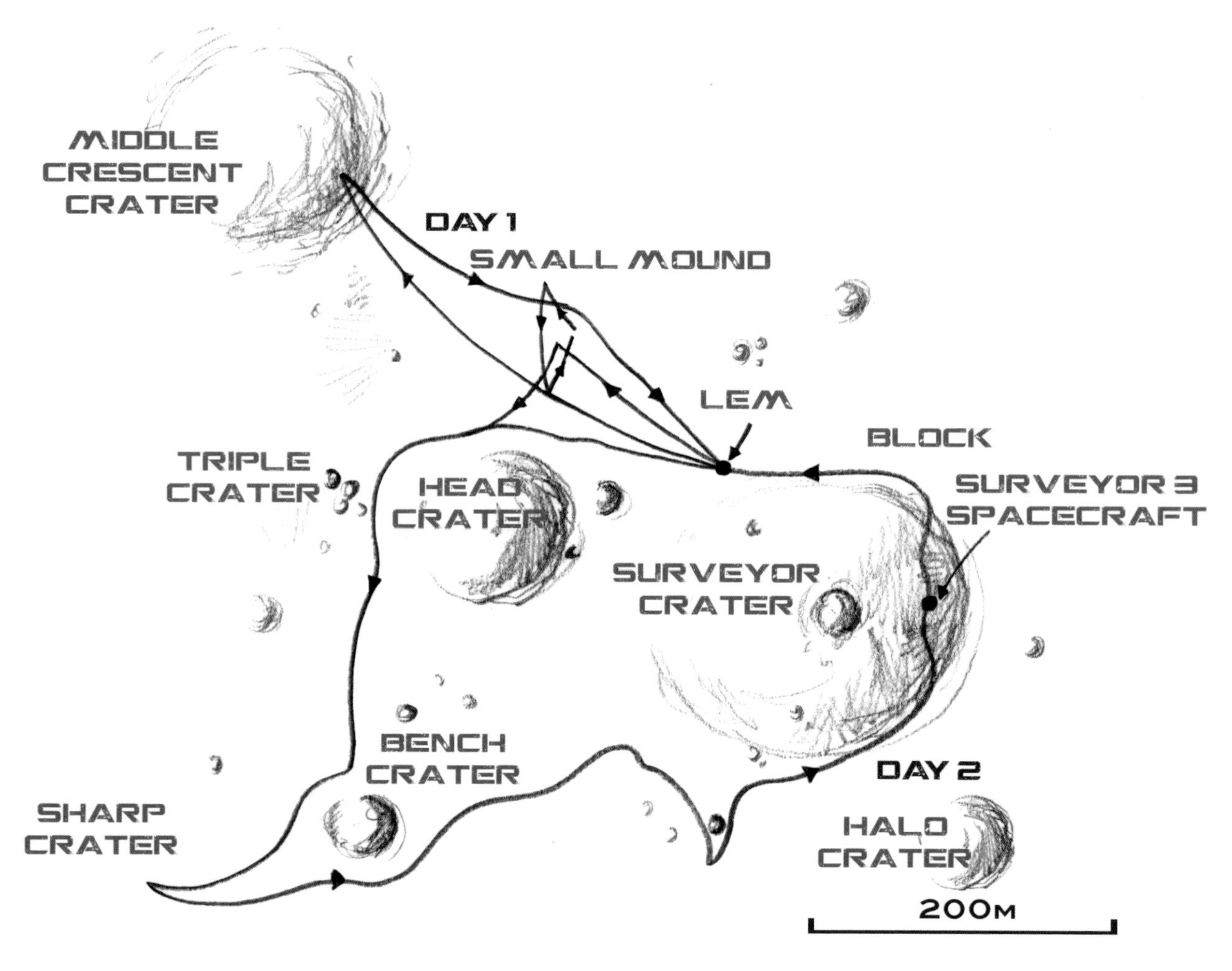

Apollo 12 landing site map

11:32AM

"Bye-bye, see you in a minute," says Al, filled with glee at what's to follow. He's been waiting six years for this moment. It's his first space flight – and he's come straight to the Moon. He can't quite believe his luck. Al's landed here on the Moon's Ocean of Storms with his dear friend Pete just four and a half hours ago, and the pair have been itching to get outside ever since. Now Pete is struggling on all fours, just as Neil did five months earlier at another landing site about 1600 kilometres to the east.

"How am I doing?" asks Pete.
"Doing good," replies Al. "You're headed right square out the hatch. Wait. Wait. Oops. Come forward a little. Move to your right. You got to kneel down a little more. I'll push you if you don't mind."

Al begins to push down on Pete's helmet to guide him cleanly out of the hatch.

"OK, I'm out on the porch," says Pete.

Just like Neil, Pete reaches for the handle, which will trigger a TV camera to fold out on its platform beneath him. Once again, it will relay his first steps on the Moon to those watching back on Earth. Pete and Al will soon become the third and fourth people to set foot on the Moon. They both know that history will only remember the first men to walk here – Neil and Buzz – but that doesn't stop them being excited. After all, it will be their first time walking on the Moon – and that's all that matters to them.

"Man, that's a heck of a tug with that handle," grumbles Pete. "Good Godfrey. That handle's in there like something I never saw before." Aware that there are thousands of kids listening to him back on Earth, Pete's keeping his language clean, throwing in playful words and phrases rather than his more usual swear words.

Below him, the first colour TV camera to reach the lunar surface swings into action. It has a spinning wheel behind the lens, with red, green and blue filters on it, beaming three different coloured frames back to Earth, where they are turned into moving colour pictures.

As Pete climbs further down the ladder, he glances off to his left and catches sight of something.

"Hey, I'll tell you what we're parked next to," he reports to Al.
"What?" asks Al excitedly.
"We're about 25 feet in front of the Surveyor Crater," says Pete.
"That's good," says Al. "That's where we wanted to be."

Pete and Al have landed in this particular spot because, three and half years earlier, an unmanned robotic spacecraft called *Surveyor 3* landed here to study the Moon's surface before any people arrived.

"I bet you when I get down to the bottom of the ladder, I can see the *Surveyor*," says Pete. "Whew! I'm heading down the ladder."

Back on Earth, the first live TV pictures are just reaching everyone's TV sets. A lucky few who have a colour television can now see Pete's feet appearing in slightly fuzzy colour.

"You're coming into the picture now, Pete," says his friend Ed Gibson on the radio from Earth.
"OK," replies Pete – the delight evident in his voice.

Pete steps down to the last rung of the ladder and then jumps off – dropping the last metre on to the footpad, his hands slipping down the outside rails to steady himself. The slowness of his fall in the reduced lunar gravity surprises him.

"Whoopie! Man, that may have been a small one for Neil, but that's a long one for me!" he cries out. Pete has made a bet with someone back on Earth that he's free to say whatever he wants when he steps on to the Moon – and he's just proved it.
"OK. I'm going to step off the pad."

Still holding the ladder, Pete sets his left foot into the lunar dirt. "Mark. Off the... Ooh, is that soft and squidgy.

"Hey, that's neat." He pauses, enjoying the sensation of standing somewhere that's not Earth.

"I don't sink in too far," he reports. Pete lets go of the ladder and steps away from the spacecraft – his hand swinging out of the shade and into the brilliant sunlight. "Boy, that Sun is bright. That's just like somebody shining a spotlight in your hand."

Pete walks stiffly a few more paces, savouring the moment of being the only living thing standing on this whole entire world. "Well, I can walk pretty well, Al, but I've got to take it easy and watch what I'm doing."

He turns and looks over towards Surveyor Crater – trying to catch sight of the robot lander.
"Boy, you'll never believe it!" Pete exclaims in delight. "Guess what I see sitting on the side of the crater!"
Al can guess alright. "The old *Surveyor*, right?"
"The old *Surveyor*. Yes, sir," Pete laughs. "Does that look neat! It can't be any further than 600 feet from here. How about that?"

Pete starts trying to collect a rock sample with his scoop. Al is watching him out of the spacecraft window. "Boy, you sure lean forward, Pete," he observes.

Pete has only been walking on the Moon a few minutes and is still adjusting.
"Hey, I feel like I'm going to fall over in any direction," he reports, leaning over.
"On Earth, you'd fall over leaning that far forward!" says Al.
"It seems a little weird, I'll tell you. Don't think you're going to steam around here quite as fast as you thought you were."

Pete soon notices that he can't really walk on the Moon. The reduced gravity prompts him to move in a lope. Walking takes more effort than loping.

While Al readies the equipment to send down to Pete on the clothes line-tether winch system that Neil and Buzz also used, Pete heads for the TV camera to set it up on a stand. Well-trained and at ease with his tasks, he starts to hum to himself in delight.

"Dum, dum, da dee da dee dum. Trying to learn to move faster." He breaks into a little run – skipping from foot to foot in a long stride. "Pretty good! Hey, I feel great!" Pete switches into more of a bunny hop.
"Dee dum dee dum. I feel like Bugs Bunny," he chuckles, heading back to help Al, who's still in the spacecraft.

Al winches the stills camera down to Pete, who retrieves it and sets it up to take photos.

"Be out in a minute," shouts Al excitedly.
"All right. Let me know so I can photograph you," replies Pete.

Secretly Pete and Al have smuggled a special camera timer to the Moon, which they hope to attach to the camera to snap a photograph standing together by *Surveyor 3*. The little device is chrome covered and shiny, but Pete can't spot it in the bag he hid it in. He doesn't want Mission Control back in Houston to know about it, so he pretends to be doing something else. He's still rummaging for it when Al starts down the ladder.

"OK, I'm ready for you," says Pete, still unable to locate the timer.
Al starts to back out of the hatch – wriggling backwards on to the porch.
Pete's watching him. "That's it. Get your knees down. That a boy. Good shape, good shape. OK."
"Pretty good," says Al, putting his hand up to adjust his helmet. "I'd better get my visor down though."
"Yes sir! My, that Sun is bright," adds Pete.

Al carries on down the ladder. "Boy," he says, "the LEM looks nice on the outside."
He drops on to the footpad.
"You look great. Welcome aboard!" says Pete.
"OK. My, that Sun is bright," says Al, speaking his first words on the Moon.
"Take it easy," warns Pete.
"It feels good," says Al, stepping off to his right.
"Yeah, you really do begin to adapt," replies Pete encouragingly.

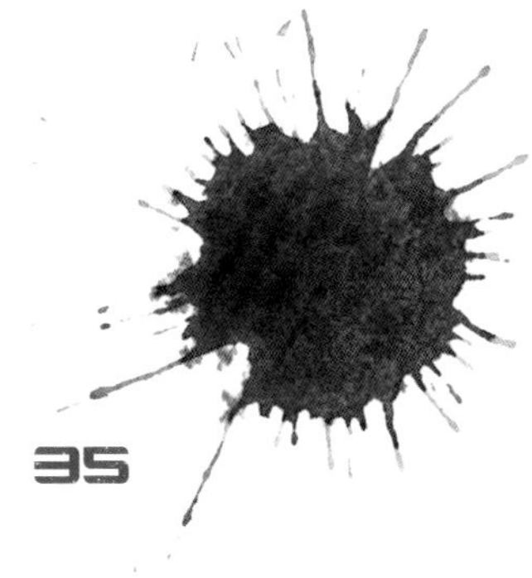

Al is immediately struck by the loneliness of the place. He looks at Pete and thinks to himself, "We're the only people around here. The whole Moon is here – and the two of us are the only things on it." It strikes him that this has never been the case on Earth because there are always other people around somewhere else on the planet. But not here on the Moon. It feels very weird to him.

But right now there's no time to contemplate this further. He already feels the pressure of their task list. The pair start to set up a dish-shaped antenna to better beam colour TV pictures back to Earth.

"Al, can you find the Earth?" asks Pete. "Where's the Earth?"*

The Earth is sitting 30 degrees above the horizon – hard to glimpse through their helmets, which don't rotate as they tip their heads back. It's only a thin crescent today and tricky to spot – just a tiny slither of Antarctica and the Persian Gulf, illuminated by the Sun.

"OK. Point to Earth," continues Pete – reading his instructions. "That's what it says."

Al is supposed to be familiarising himself with moving around on the Moon's surface, but Pete is keen to put him to work setting up the antenna. Although they have practised this back on Earth, it seems to be more of a struggle up here. As they unpack it, they delight in throwing the packaging as far as they can. In the airless vacuum even the lightest, flappiest bits of packaging travel as far as a rock being thrown on Earth, as if flying away under their own steam.

* Because the Moon always points the same face towards the Earth, the Earth always appears fixed in the same position in the Moon's sky – its height above the horizon dependent on where on the Moon you are standing. If you were standing in the dead centre of the Moon, as we see it from Earth, it would be right overhead, but from here, where Pete and Al have landed, off to the side a little, the Earth's fixed permanently in the same position in the sky – 30 degrees above the horizon to the east. It doesn't rise or set like the Sun and Moon appear to do from Earth. Instead it just hangs there, locked in the same position of the Moon's black sky. But it does display phases like the Moon, sometimes presenting a fully illuminated face and other times – like the day Pete and Al are there – a thin crescent.

"OK, Houston, I'm about to move the TV camera now," calls Al. He hops over to where Pete's left it on the spacecraft. "Hey, it's real nice moving around up here. You don't seem to get tired. You really hop like a bunny."

As Al retrieves the camera and carries it over to the right position to set it up, he accidentally points it straight at the Sun, frying its electronics. Even with the bigger dish antenna they've set up now streaming its pictures back to Earth, no one can see a thing. The global TV audience of eager moonwalk watchers will have to make do with just the sound of Pete and Al's running commentary from now on, to follow the adventure.

As the pair go about their work, Al has more fun jettisoning the styrofoam packaging that some of the experiments have come wrapped in.

"Look at that, Pete," he cries, launching another piece high into the air, amazed at just how long it takes to come back down.

Mindful that now, with the TV camera broken, no one on Earth can see the fun, Al describes what he's doing.

"Hey, one of the fun things here, Houston, is all these styrofoam packing blocks that are put on there to protect it during shipment or launch. When you take them off and throw them, they really sail. These things stay airborne for 10 seconds, maybe."

Eager to engage Pete with the thrill of the packaging hurling, Al tries to distract him again.
"Hey, Pete? Pete?" he cries.
"What?" replies Pete without looking up.
"Watch this," shouts Al, hurling another piece of styrofoam packaging as far into the distance as he can. It seems to defy gravity – staying aloft for far longer than it would on Earth.
"It hasn't hit the ground yet," marvels Al, "it might have gone up 300 feet."

Pete, now fully enthralled in Al's game of chuck the packaging, laughs heartily.

"Boing!" cries Al – adding his own sound effect as the block hits the ground again.
Still laughing, Pete suddenly remembers that they're behind with their task list.

"Stop playing and get to work. Come on," he chuckles, incredulous that the two of them are actually larking about ON THE MOON! "Maybe they'll extend us to four and a half hours," he continues, hoping Mission Control will allow them more time outside. "I feel like I could stay out here all day!"

Pete snaps a couple of pictures of Al at work, the Moon's morning sunshine illuminating his bright white spacesuit against the inky blackness of the lunar sky.

"Houston, how long you going to let us stay out?"
A minute of silence crackles back through the vacuum.
Pete tries again.
"Hello, Houston?"

"Al, Houston. Go ahead," says Ed, mistaking Pete for Al.

"OK. How long you going to let us stay out?" repeats Pete.

Ed takes some time to confirm the answer.

"Pete, you'll be extended 30 minutes, so you're out for a total of four hours."

"Hey, man!" replies Al with glee.

"You've got about one hour left," Ed confirms.

Ed suggests that the two of them head for a large crater, known as Middle Crescent, about 100 metres to the northwest. Al and Pete start the walk, searching for rock samples to collect along the way.

It takes them about 15 minutes to get there.

"We're almost over to the thousand-foot crater," says Pete. "Got about another 200 feet to go."

Back on Earth, Ed and his friends are paying close attention to how much oxygen, cooling water and power Pete and Al have got left. Strict rules are in place to make sure they don't run too low while outside the spacecraft on their moonwalk, or EVA as they call it – standing for Extra Vehicular Activity.

"We show you're 3 hours and 7 minutes into the EVA," says Ed. "And we'd like you back to the LEM to start the closeout in 10 minutes. That's at 3 plus 17."

"Holy Christmas," says Pete, still trying his best to keep his language clean. "We're going to have to smoke there Houston. We're not getting very many rocks by going this far. But if that's what you want, that's what you want," he laughs. "Run, baby!"

As they both quicken their pace, skipping across the Moon, Al's heart rate hits 140 beats a minute and Pete's rises to 150.

As Al races over the Moon, he occasionally looks up to the east and spies the Earth hanging there in the black sky. "That's the Earth, and this is the Moon," he says to himself, not really able to fully grasp the enormity of where he is. Earth seems so far away. He thinks about it some more. But then the burden of all the tasks on his to-do list, sewn on to the left cuff of his suit, snaps him back to the job in hand. Al worries a lot in life. He worries what people think of him. He worries about his friends and letting his team down. He's always anxious to do his very best. Perhaps it's this conscientious approach that's helped to get him to the Moon.

As they get closer to Middle Crescent Crater, it stretches out impressively ahead of them.

"Look at that!" cries Pete. "That crater's spectacular isn't it? Wow, a monster!"
"Look at that rock!" shouts Al. "I'd like to get some of this bedrock!"

Bedrock is a geologist's dream. It's rock that's still attached to the ground, and not broken off or moved, so it's clear where it came from. Neil and Buzz only managed to find rubble at their landing site, which could have come from almost anywhere on the Moon. Pristine, undisturbed bedrock is just what Pete and Al are looking for.

With their time on the surface running out, the two astronauts rush to photograph the big crater and collect samples.

"Al. We suggest that you hustle," says Ed. "We show you're 3 hours and 11 minutes, and we'd like you back there around 3 hours 17 minutes. Six more minutes."

"We're picking up a couple right now, and we're on our way back," reports Al.

He scans the scene, looking for bedrock, when something suddenly catches his eye. "Just a minute… Boy! There's a big block over there," he says.

Pete bounds towards it, reaching over to try to pick it up.

"Can't get it," he mutters, straining to grab it.

He makes another attempt, using a grab arm, trying to lift it off the ground.
"Got it?" asks Al.
"I can't get it with the tongs," replies Pete in frustration.
"Hold my hand and pick it up," suggests Al, hoping to help Pete keep his balance as he leans over to get the rock. Pete grabs Al's hand and tries again.

CHAPTER 02

Still struggling, Al suggests Pete push it his way so he can grab it himself. Working together, they just get hold of it in the nick of time.

"Pete and Al. We suggest you start smoking on back there," advises Ed. "You're 3:13 and I'd like you back there in four minutes."

"OK. We're on our way," replies Pete. "Let's go, Al."

Six minutes later, the two of them are back at their spacecraft, a little puffed.

"Hey, Houston. We're back at the LEM," reports Pete, trying to catch his breath. "Not going to have any trouble sleeping tonight!"

Back inside the LEM, Al and Pete close the door, fill the cabin with air again and then take their helmets off and recharge their life support backpacks. They start to prepare their supper. Before they left Earth, the astronauts chose what food they'd like to eat each day. Al chose spaghetti for his first meal on the Moon! It's his favourite food.

Al eats it every day for lunch on Earth and NASA has supplied him with a tasty spaghetti and meat sauce dish for tonight. It's cold as there's no way to heat up their food inside the spaceship – but Al is happy nonetheless. They might not be the first people to visit the Moon, but Al is delighted to be the first person to eat spaghetti on the Moon.

He follows it up with a dessert of peaches, all washed down with an orange and grapefruit drink called TANG, which is made from a powder. Pete also dines on spaghetti and meat sauce, followed by banana dessert, washed down with a grape punch drink.

Outside, the long 708 hour lunar day rolls on – the Sun still rising towards midday. But Pete and Al are Earth creatures who sleep for eight hours in every 24. After feasting, the pair draw down blinds on the spaceship's small windows, string up a couple of hammocks and prepare to sleep. They've been awake for almost 18 hours and have had a very busy day.
Tomorrow will be even busier.

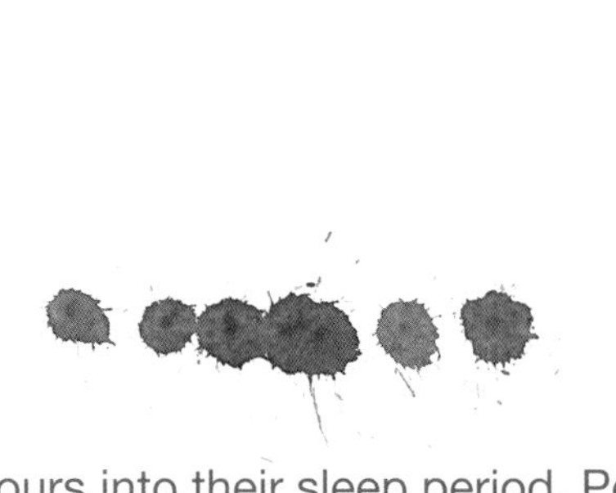

About five hours into their sleep period, Pete's suit becomes so uncomfortable that it wakes him up. Both men know they are unlikely to be back this way again. They need to make the most of their time here, so they put the blinds up and start preparing to go outside for the final time.

Back on Earth, Ed's colleague Paul has taken over to wake the crew. "Good morning," he says. "How did you sleep?"

"Short, but sweet," replies Pete. "We're hustling right now. We're going to eat breakfast, have a little talk with you, and get about our business."

Two hours later, both men are climbing back out the hatch – ready for another busy day working on the Moon.

"Whoops, long step," hollers Pete as he drops down the ladder once more.
"OK, Houston. Mark. I'm on the lunar surface."

It is still the same lunar 'day' outside, but it feels like a new one to Pete after his sleep.
"Almost cold today," he announces, standing in the chill of the spacecraft's shadow.

Although there's no air around him to be warm or cold, the temperature of the ground and the ladder he's holding on to is 150 degrees below the freezing point of water. But the cold Pete's feeling is not coming from outside. The suit he's wearing has 26 layers of protective material to keep him at the optimum temperature wherever he's standing. He's feeling cold because he's got the temperature inside it set to mid-cooling. It's time warm it up a bit.

Their tasks today are to take a walk anticlockwise in a loop around the landing site, taking in five more craters and ending up at the largest – Surveyor Crater – where the robot they've come to visit sits.

They're carrying with them a kind of metal crate that holds the hand tools and sample bags they'll be using to store any rocks they collect. It's an awkward contraption to lug around and tends to bump into their knees as they walk. This can be avoided by holding it out a bit further, but the more rock samples they load on to it the heavier it gets, making their arms ache. They take it in turns to haul it from crater to crater. The next expedition to the Moon will bring one with wheels to make life a bit easier. But Pete and Al are stuck with lugging this one.

"OK. Al, where's the map?" asks Pete.
"Got the map right here, Pete. Why don't you take a look at this?"

Before coming to the Moon, Pete and Al requested a map to help them navigate to each crater they're supposed to visit. Down on the ground, one crater looks very much like another, but thanks to the map they've got a better idea of which is which.

"This is the smartest idea we came up with, Houston," reports Pete, feeling pleased with their decision to bring it. "This map just works great out here."

The pair head off south in search of more bedrock – perhaps exposed in the crater walls.

As they enter a modest-sized crater called Sharp, their feet start to sink into the squashy ground.

"It's awful soft in here; watch it," warns Pete. "Holy Christmas! Look at the bottom of that," he continues, drawing Al's attention to blast marks etched into the floor of the crater. "This has got to be fairly fresh, look at that, Al. Isn't that neat?"

Sharp is a depression about 18 metres across, easily wide enough to park a school bus inside. It formed in an instant when a large piece of rock and ice, travelling at several tens of kilometres a second, smacked into the Moon.

Pete starts snapping photos of the crater. It's a dramatic reminder that the Moon's battered surface has been shaped by trillions of such impacts over billions of years. How lucky we all are to live on Earth – where most rocks from space burn up in the atmosphere before smashing into the ground.

They gather some rock samples and press on eastwards – now facing into the Sun. Even with their gold visors down, the strong light dazzles them, making it hard to avoid stepping into holes and pits in the undulating ground.

"You know what I feel like, Al?" asks Pete as the pair of them lope along.

"What?" says Al.
"Did you ever see those pictures of giraffes running in slow motion?" chuckles Pete.
"That's about right," agrees Al.

"That's exactly what I feel like," giggles Pete.

Ed is listening in again back on Earth.
"Say, would you giraffes give us some comment on your boot penetration as you move across there, and what you had back there at Sharp Crater?" he asks.

"Oh, it's much firmer here," reports Pete. "We don't sink in anywhere near as much."
"Yeah," agrees Al. "The toes sink in a bit Pete, as you push off. You land flat-footed, so your heels don't sink in, but as you push off with your toes, they sink in – down about three inches. Your heels are only sunk in perhaps an eighth of an inch."

Al's watchlng Pete running ahead of him – the bright sunlight backlighting his friend's footsteps.

"Every time Pete lands he sends little particles spraying out ahead of him and beside him and everywhere else," Al radios to Ed, marvelling at the spectacle. "They go out to distances maybe two feet to three feet around him."

Pete and Al press on east – now leaping along at about four kilometres an hour. They are taking it in turns to lug the crate with them as they head towards another crater called Halo Crater. Both men are getting tired and out of breath, and before long they need to take a break.

"I've got the decided feeling I'm going to sleep tonight," says Pete. "Tell you one thing I'd go for is a good drink of ice water," he adds, wishing they had a way of quenching their thirst.*

After a short rest they press on.

"Continue directly east right into the Sun," Ed advises, trying to give them clear directions. "And then at 9 o'clock you'll see the LEM," he continues, referring to a clock face where 12 o'clock is north. "A couple more steps and you'll be there."

* Future space suits designed for spending longer out on the Moon will have a drinking straw positioned inside their helmets, near their mouths, connected to a bag filled with liquid that they can suck on. But Pete and Al don't have such a luxury.

They eventually make it to Halo Crater, collect some more samples and take photos before heading north again towards their final destination – Surveyor Crater – and their rendezvous with the robot.

The Sun is now to their right, making it easier to race across the lunar surface, and both men up their pace.

Suddenly Al's ears pop. The sensation stops him in his tracks. An abrupt change in pressure means only one thing to him: a leak in his suit. It's every astronaut's worst nightmare. Al tenses up, waiting for more signs of pressure change. But he feels nothing. His air pressure gauge still reads normal. Ed hasn't picked up anything unusual back on Earth. Could he have imagined it? It felt real enough. He pushes on to keep up with Pete, and tries to forget about it.**

** Back on Earth after the flight, mission controllers work out what had happened. An exhaust valve in Al's suit, designed to let out excess air, had pressed up against his belly as he ran, blocking it up and causing the pressure to rise and his ears to pop. When he stopped running, it bounced back off his belly – releasing the excess air out again and returning the air pressure to normal. Before the next flight to the Moon, NASA put a little wire basket over the inside of it, to stop it ever blocking up again.

As they approach Surveyor Crater, both men are getting excited. It's the largest crater they've seen here on the Moon – maybe 15 times as large as Sharp. And there, on the crater's eastern slopes, squats their trusty robot – its three feet dug into the dust where it touched down over three years ago.

Although Pete and Al never met *Surveyor 3* before it left Earth, they're familiar with a full-scale model of the machine. They've been training with it back on Earth. But seeing the real robot here for the first time, sitting at a slight angle on the crater's slopes, is a wonderful moment. Designed to take pictures and dig a trench with a robotic arm to test the properties of the Moon's surface, *Surveyor 3* hasn't moved for three years, its batteries now dead. But it still makes a great sight.

"I tell you what, why don't you get a photograph of it right now?" suggests Pete.
"It's a good place," agrees Al.
"OK. Will do. Stop and do it right here."

Pete is transfixed by it. "Look. You can see which way it came in. See the way this gear pad dug in over there..." he observes, fascinated by how it landed itself here all those years before, bouncing a little as it touched down and then sliding slightly down the crater's slope.

"Yeah. It's going to make a good shot," says Al.
"Beautiful. Beautiful sight."

As they approach the craft it towers over them, a solar panel 'top hat' it wears rising high into the black sky above. It makes an imposing presence. Pete and Al have planned to snap a selfie posing with the robot. But the secret camera timer they've smuggled up here to take the shot is still lost. Both of them look through the various bags of equipment they're carrying one last time.

"Wait a minute," says Pete, thinking he's found it. "What's in your bag, here?" He continues to rummage – but only comes out with a roll of film. They've both practised trying to find it back on Earth – but here on the Moon, the inside of the bags are darker and their thick gloves aren't helping them to locate it.

Reluctantly the pair give up the search – snapping individual portraits of each other by the *Surveyor* instead. The robot has a camera onboard, which took pictures of the trench it dug, and their last job is to cut this off and return it to Earth to study how it's been affected by the Moon's environment.*

"Let me get a grip on it now," says Al, reaching out to grasp the camera.
"OK," says Pete excitedly. "That's ours!"
"We got her!" declares Al, cutting it off.
"Beautiful!" says Pete.
"OK. I think I can hold that with one hand and open the bag," says Al holding up a nylon bag. "Get in there. Get in that bag!" Al cries – willing it in.
"There you go. In the bag! In the bag!"
"Good show," says Pete encouragingly.

"Copy. It's in the bag," chimes in Ed, listening attentively from Earth. "Well done, troops."

With this last task complete, Pete and Al head back to the spaceship. Their final walk on the Moon is almost over. Despite his exhaustion, Pete is still determined to have a little fun.

In his final moments on the Moon, he attempts an aerial pirouette – leaping off the ground and spinning his body as fast as he dare. To his delight, he manages a half turn before landing again.

"Oh, this is so much fun," he laughs in delight. "I can jump up about three feet and do a 180. See if I can do a 360!"

* When *Surveyor 3* was being assembled on Earth, great care was taken not to contaminate it with any bugs from Earth. But, when Pete and Al brought the camera back after three years exposed to the vacuum of space and the extreme heat of the lunar day and cold of the lunar night, to everyone's surprise, bacteria were found inside it. For 30 years it was thought they'd survived on the Moon all that time – until further analysis in 2011 suggested that the bugs might in fact have come from the bag Al dropped the camera into, or the labs that analysed it back on Earth. The lesson of this story is just how hard it is to search for life on other planets in our solar system without contaminating the results from Earth, where life is everywhere.

He tries again, but this time his bulky life support backpack carries on after he comes down, pulling him off balance.
"You got to watch it though," he warns.
"You get all that mass going around and you get in trouble."
"OK," says Al, just happy to watch his best friend larking about here in front of him.

The pair of them are covered in moon dust from their two days of exploring. The black dirt has turned their once pristine white space suits to a light grey.

"Gotta brush you off," Pete reminds Al, trying to prevent too much dust making it into their spacecraft. "Why don't you hop up on the ladder and let me brush you off?"

Both astronauts attempt to clean the other. But the dust is hard to shift. With no water or wind to smooth the rocks on the Moon, the lunar dust is made up of fine jagged pieces. And as Neil and Buzz found, it's very sticky too – thanks to all the electrical charge it carries. It makes brushing the stuff off their suits almost impossible.

With as much dust removed as possible, Al jumps up to the first rung of the ladder, banging his boots against the spacecraft in a final attempt to knock off any last bits of dirt.

Just as Pete's about to start up the ladder, he checks something with Al.
"Did you ever get the picture of the LEM and Earth?" he asks.
"Nope," replies Al.
"Oh, that's a shame," says Pete.
"I know it," admits Al, still regretting breaking the TV camera when they'd first arrived.

Knowing there's no photo of this special view, Pete makes one final effort to see it for himself, arching backwards to try to catch sight of his home planet from the surface of the Moon for the last time.
"Hi, Earth! I can see us," he cries, his mind already back there on the world he belongs to.

It's time to head home.

CHAPTER 03

Fra Mauro Formation
Saturday February 6th 1971

On the surface of the moon
Al Shepard CDR
(Commander)
Ed Mitchell LMP
(Lunar Module Pilot)

Voice from earth
Fred Haise CAPCOM (Capsule Communicator)

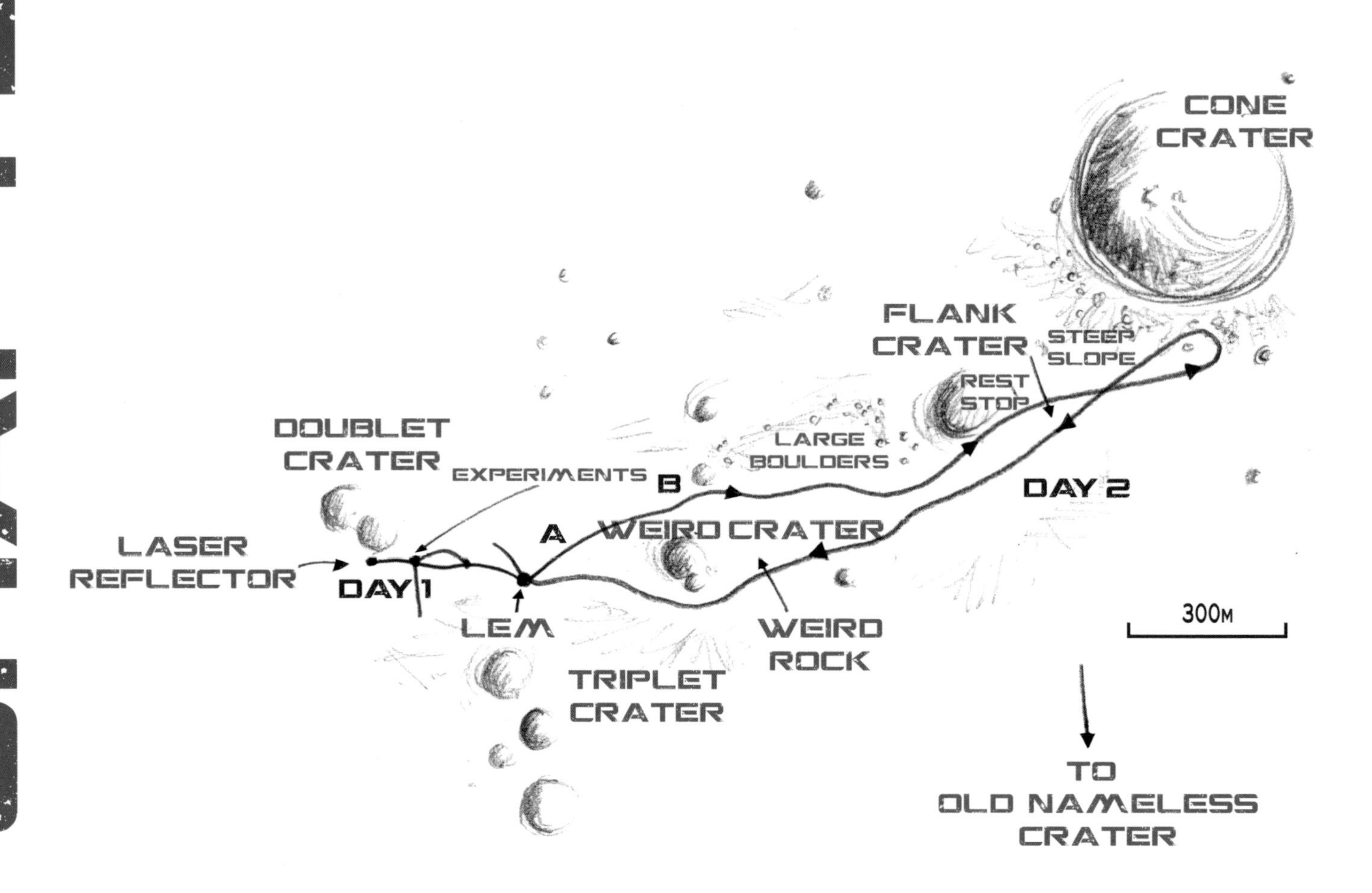

Apollo 14 landing Site map

9:35AM

"Well, where do you think we are?" asks Al.

Alan Shepard is the second man named Al to walk on the Moon. He's also the oldest person ever to set foot here. Two and a half months ago he turned 47. Al was born in 1923, a mere 20 years after the very first aeroplane flight was made on Earth. By the time he was just 36 years old, he'd become the first American to fly into space, and here he is, only 11 years later, having flown to the Moon! The speed of human progress that's placed him here feels breathtaking.

"Can you see the boulders off to the side there on the map?" asks his pal Ed, studying a photograph of their location taken from orbit.

Al and Ed landed their spaceship – called *Antares* – here yesterday, just 1.3 kilometres west of a giant chasm in the Moon's surface called Cone Crater. The two of them have already spent a day exploring the area around the spacecraft, laying out experiments like those who visited the Moon before them.

But today they're attempting a first. They're going to walk all the way to Cone Crater and back. It's a hike that will take them further than any astronaut's ever been away from their spacecraft. And right now it's not going so well. In fact they're lost.

Ed continues, trying to make sense of the map.
"You should be able to spot that little chain of craters just to the south of us on the map, if that's where we think we are," he reasons.
"Boy, that little chain of craters right there..." replies Al.
"Kind of small," notes Ed.
"That will make us right here, huh?" asks Al.

It's been over a year since the last humans walked on the Moon – and that's because in April last year, the third attempt almost ended in disaster when a faulty oxygen tank onboard the spacecraft exploded. It had been a reminder of just how hard and dangerous it is for humans to come here.

Thankfully the crew on that mission – Jim Lovell, John Swigert and Fred Haise – all made it back to Earth safely; but it took the rest of the year to work out what had gone wrong, and to make sure it didn't happen again. Al and Ed are relieved to be here after all that, and they're excited about their hike to the giant crater today.

To carry everything they need for the longest moonwalk in history, the pair are hauling a two-wheeled trolley behind them. It's known as the MET – standing for Modular Equipment Transporter. It's laden down with instruments, tools and sample collection bags, and it's leaving deep tyre tracks in the fine lunar dust behind them. These are the first wheel marks ever made on the Moon. The sight reminds them of tracks in fresh snow.

In fact, the whole pristine lunar surface reminds them of a big snow scene. "You're ready to go out and play in the snow?" Al had asked Ed, as they got ready to step on to the Moon for the first time yesterday.
"Yeah, it looks like my snowsuit's ready," Ed had replied.

But now – a day later – they're lost in this 'snow scape'. Ed is carrying a map of the area – made from photographs of their landing site taken from orbit by an earlier mission. He's stopping regularly to try to match it to the features he's seeing around him. But it's not easy. From ground level, the area seems very flat and featureless.

One of the experiments they did yesterday revealed that the dust around here is eight metres deep – almost enough to bury a three-storey house. All this dust has accumulated through billions of years of impacts from space rocks raining down on to the Moon and pulverising the surface.

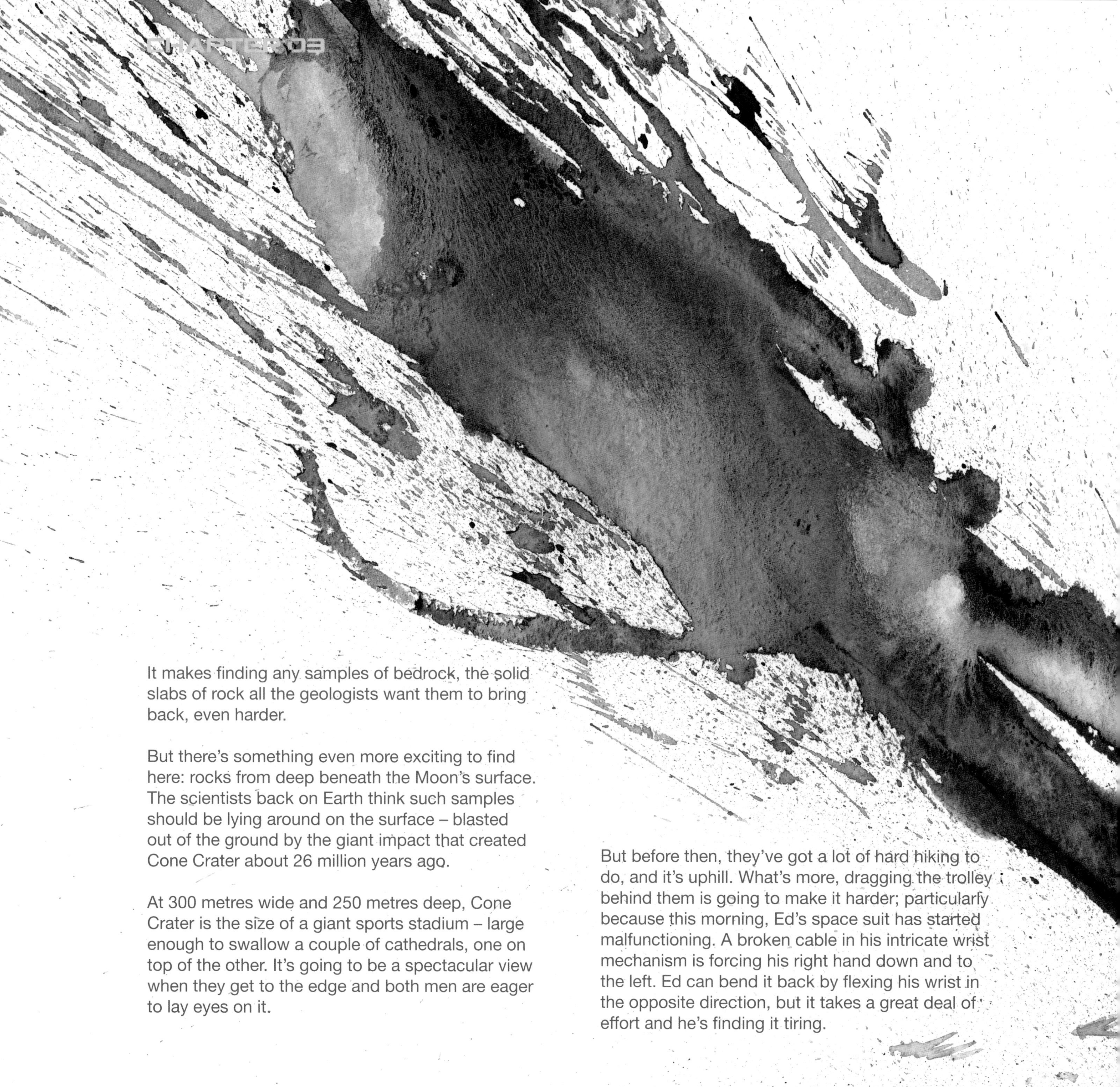

It makes finding any samples of bedrock, the solid slabs of rock all the geologists want them to bring back, even harder.

But there's something even more exciting to find here: rocks from deep beneath the Moon's surface. The scientists back on Earth think such samples should be lying around on the surface – blasted out of the ground by the giant impact that created Cone Crater about 26 million years ago.

At 300 metres wide and 250 metres deep, Cone Crater is the size of a giant sports stadium – large enough to swallow a couple of cathedrals, one on top of the other. It's going to be a spectacular view when they get to the edge and both men are eager to lay eyes on it.

But before then, they've got a lot of hard hiking to do, and it's uphill. What's more, dragging the trolley behind them is going to make it harder; particularly because this morning, Ed's space suit has started malfunctioning. A broken cable in his intricate wrist mechanism is forcing his right hand down and to the left. Ed can bend it back by flexing his wrist in the opposite direction, but it takes a great deal of effort and he's finding it tiring.

Despite these setbacks, Ed's determined that his last day on the Moon won't be spoiled. He loves walking on the Moon and likens it to walking on a trampoline. With relatively little effort, he can glide across the surface in long high steps. He's settled on leaping along in a sort of two-footed bunny hop – landing on his right foot and then pushing off with his left foot slightly ahead of his right. With each bound, he almost feels as if he's levitating – walking on air. It gives him a euphoric feeling. Walking on the Moon is so easy.
But navigating is much harder.

On Earth, the atmosphere gives us clues to how far away something is – more distant objects becoming fainter, hidden in the haze. But here on the Moon, with no air to look through, everything appears super sharp and much closer than it really is; whether it's a nearby rock or a very distant crater. The only object they know the true size of is their spacecraft, which they can still see in the distance behind them. Ed starts holding his thumb up to it to gauge its apparent size at this distance. But it's not a very useful guide.

The lack of atmosphere makes accurate navigation by eye almost impossible. But this is not their only problem. Every time the trolley they're pulling hits a slight rise in the ground, or a rock, it takes off about half a metre and threatens to tip over. It needs all their skill and persistence to keep it stable.

The TV camera they set up back at the spacecraft is pointing in the direction they're heading, but the image it's beaming back to Earth is so fuzzy that soon the two of them have disappeared from view.

Now Fred Haise, their support buddy back on Earth, can only monitor their progress by listening in on their conversation.

"Think we ought to check our position right about here, Al," suggests Ed. "See if we can find out where we are."
"There seem to be quite a few large rocks as we progress along here," he continues. "I see rocks of up to two or three feet in size, and one would fairly easily postulate these came directly from Cone Crater.
"Rog," replies Fred. Fred was on the ill-fated Moon flight last year that nearly ended in disaster and never reached the lunar surface. But he spent a year training to walk here and knows the place really well. He's a good person to have on the other end of the radio, in case things go wrong.

Like Ed, Fred also has a map of their landing site, made from photos taken from above. He's using it to help steer them towards Cone Crater, by taking bearings from other landmarks he can see on the photo.

"Any basic change in the surface texture as you're heading out?" he asks. The science team on Earth is expecting some big changes in the terrain as they get closer to the site of the giant impact.

"No. It looks all the same, Fredo," replies Ed.

"That's what I was afraid of," continues Fred, concerned that they're already heading off course – skirting around Cone Crater rather than advancing towards it.

Eager to get them back on track, Fred tries a different approach. "The blocks you described as you moved across there – do they appear to be in the form of rays from Cone or are they pretty widely spread?" he asks, hoping they might be aligned in blast lines which could help point them towards the centre of the crater.

"No. We don't see any ray pattern, I would say," reports Al. "They're fairly generally scattered."

Assuming they're at a sharply defined crater marked with a letter A on the map, Al decides they've reached the first waypoint. "How about right here. Buy that?" he asks.

"Well, it's pretty close," agrees Ed, consulting the map. "I don't think it's exactly at 'A', but it's close."

"OK, I'll clock you at 'A', right now," agrees Fred, listening in from Earth.

The two of them collect some samples from where they think they're standing at point 'A', and Al starts describing the ground.

"Fred, the surface here is textured," he begins, peering down at the fine, fresh, snow-like dust he's standing in. It's much like the dusty ground around their spacecraft. But there is something distinctly different here. "There seem to be small pebbles," he continues, noticing more debris that perhaps rained down here from the impact.

If they're where they think they are, both astronauts are about to reach a dramatic change in the texture of the ground as they cross on to a blanket of material ejected from the explosion of the impact.

"OK, Houston," begins Al, addressing Fred. "I'm looking for a contact somewhere in here, but it's not apparent at this point," he reports. "Surface texture seems to be very much the same; it's still about the same softness, and it still has the same raindrop pattern."

They carry on a little – looking for point 'B' on the map. Neither man is convinced of exactly where they are. What makes the navigating here on the Moon even harder is the roughness of the undulating ground, which regularly rises and falls three to five metres, like an ocean of frozen waves or sand dunes. It's hiding the landmarks they're both trying to spot.

Then suddenly, on the top of one of the undulations, something catches Ed's eye. "I see a string of boulders to the south of us that may prove to be a ray pattern from Cone," he reports excitedly. "And as we get closer to Cone, the number of large boulders is increasing – a dozen of them or so are four or five feet in diameter. Can you see the boulders off to the side there on the map?" he asks Al.

Al comes over to where Ed is standing, to compare their map to the view in front of them.

"Well, they don't show very well," he says, not convinced of their position.

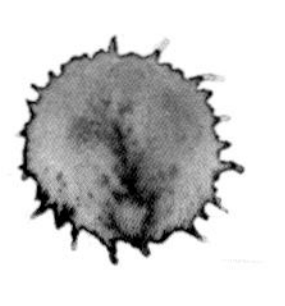

"There's no big one to go with it. No sharp one to go with it," he points out, disagreeing with Ed about where he thinks they are. "What about one right up there. How about that?" he proposes.

"Well, let's take a look," says Ed, heading off again. "That's Weird Crater, that big one right over there Al," he says, pointing to a strange heart-shaped crater about 90 metres to the south.

"Yeah. I think 'B' is that deep crater right directly ahead of us, Ed," replies Al pointing it out.

"No, I disagree," says Ed. "I think... See that crater right over there that we came by? To the south, the big one?"

"Yep," says Al.

"I think this is the crater that's 'B'," says Ed.

"This crater right here?" says Al.

"Yep. We have to be considerably past Weird," says Ed.

"Not even halfway to the rim of Cone yet," concludes Al.

"I don't think you have to worry too much about the exact position of site 'B'..." interrupts Fred.

He's concerned about how long it's taking them to pinpoint their position, and he's trying to help them from Earth, "… if it appears you're getting close to the general area, that should be good enough on 'B'."

"OK. I think we're very close to it," confirms Ed. "I think this crater we just went by is probably it, but it's very hard to tell, Fredo. I don't see anything else that might be it, unless it's the next crater up."

Ed takes another look at the map, and then up to where they're heading. "Ah, Al, I've spotted it. That next crater up is this one right here."

The two men get busy taking samples and photographing the location. They're standing on a relatively high point – about halfway up the slope leading to the edge of Cone Crater.

"The area here is in an area of considerably more boulders," reports Ed. "It's a larger boulder field; more numerous boulders than we've seen in the past. And doggone it, they may turn out to be a ray pattern. It looks suspiciously like one."

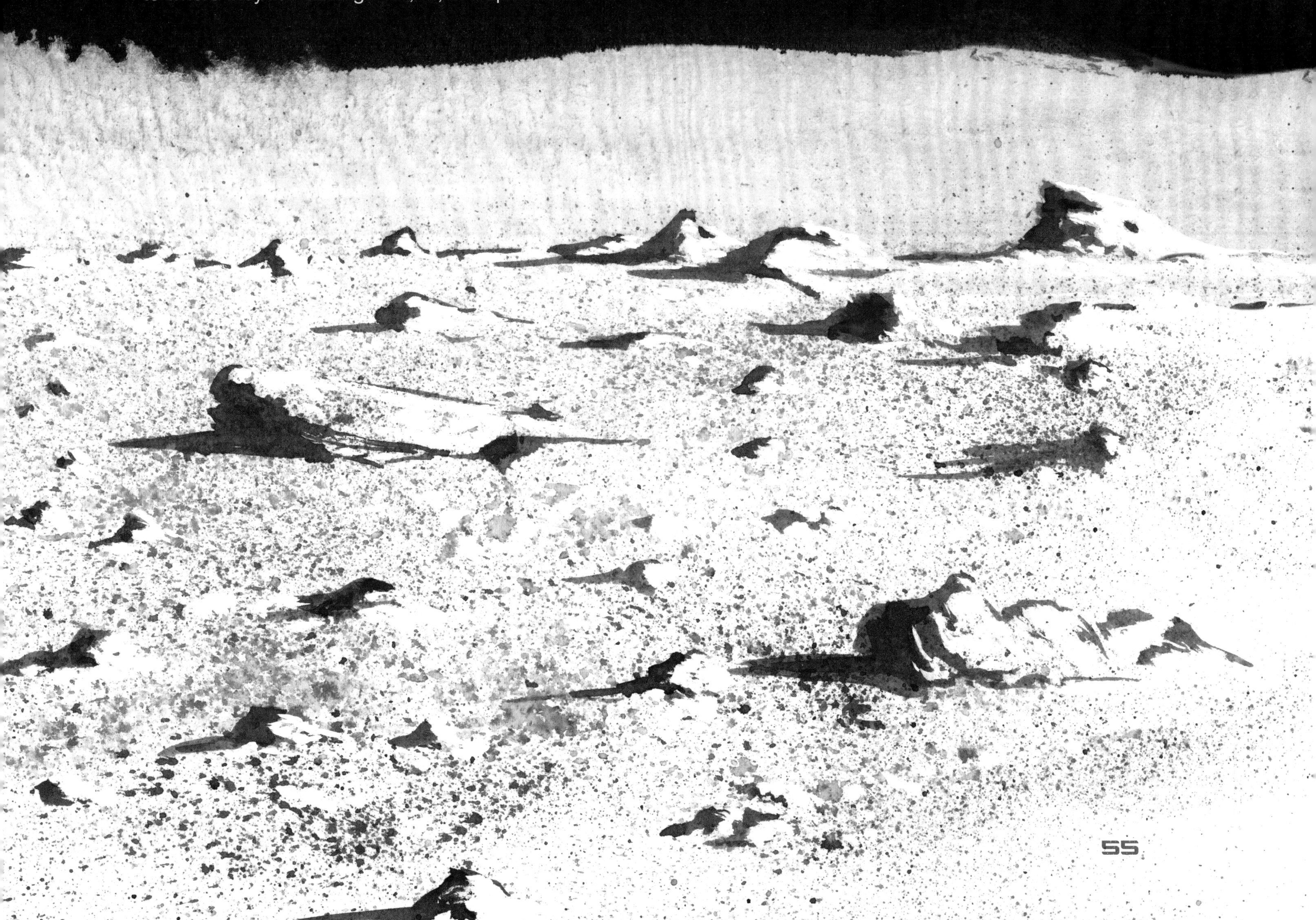

The large boulders surrounding them have probably been sitting here for 26 million years, and during that time they've continued to be bombarded by lots of smaller pieces of rock and ice, which constantly rain down on the Moon. This onslaught has rounded and smoothed most of them, but sometimes it's also smashed them into smaller angular pieces. Al is keen to grab a sample to take back for the geologists on Earth to study this process.

Fred reminds them that, at this point, they're about 15 minutes behind their timeline. It's to be expected, given the challenge of navigating here – but Ed is confident they'll catch up later. Al is not so sure.

Ed gives a last description of the view they've got, and the pair secure everything to the MET trolley and press on towards the top of Cone Crater. The climb is getting steeper and hauling the trolley is getting harder. Ed appears to be struggling a little, and is breathing heavily.

"Let me pull it for a while," offers Al, also a little puffed.
"I have to shift hands. I'm good," replies Ed.
"OK, baby! OK, I got it," says Al.
"Almost turned, didn't it," says Ed.

They press on, passing more and more small craters, some with glassy rubble in the bottom. Some seem very fresh with crisp, sharp edges. About 625 metres away from their spacecraft, they stop again to have a rest, take some more photos and check the map. Ed glances back down the slope they've climbed and spots their spaceship in the distance. It's listing to one side due to the slope they've landed on.

"That old LEM looks like it's got a flat [tyre] over there, the way it's leaning," he observes.

His gaze returns to the map – and he turns to face the Sun – tilting the map towards the strong light to get a better look and figure out where they are.

Al has got his breath back now. "OK. Start on up toward the rim?" he asks, checking if Ed is ready.
"Yeah. Just one second, though, I think I got us," replies Ed, confident with his latest navigation.
"OK, I'll head on out," replies Al, setting off up the steepening slope with the trolley in tow. It's increasingly hard work, and his heart rate soon rises to 120 beats per minute.

A few minutes later, Ed catches him up. "Let me pull awhile, Al. You're having all the fun!"
"Well, we still have a little way to go," says Al, happy to let Ed take over.
"Yes. We sure do," acknowledges Ed, grabbing the trolley. "And the grade is getting pretty steep."

Al, now following Ed, reaches forward and picks up the back of the trolley to help him carry it up the steepest bit. Together they lift it over this part of the slope.

"Left, right, left, right," calls out Al, coordinating their team effort. "Left, right, left, right."

Moving faster by working together, Ed and Al make it up another few metres, but the effort leaves them panting.

"OK. You want to rest here by this rock?" asks Al.
"OK," says Ed, pleased to stop for a bit.

"This is the first big boulder we've seen, Houston," reports Al – spotting the biggest boulder he's seen so far. "I think it's worthwhile taking a close-up picture of it."

"We probably ought to take a pan to locate everything here," suggests Ed, stopping to snap the dramatic panoramic view they have from up here. There, laid out in front of him, is a large crater called Old Nameless. With no air to distort the view it feels like it's only a couple of hundred metres from them, but incredibly it's more like two kilometres away.

They set off again for their final push.

"OK. We're starting up the last flank of the crater now, Houston," reports Ed, estimating that the slope is now climbing about a metre higher for every six metres he walks.

It's still hard going with the trolley – but the prize of the most incredible view they'll ever see is keeping them motivated. Ed notices an increase in the number of smaller rocks he's stepping on, hopefully signalling their proximity to the crater.

Al is further ahead and also spies something encouraging. “There’s the crater up there, Ed,” he cries in relief.
“Yeah. Pardon?” says Ed, tiring.

“Crater up here,” repeats Al, breathing heavily with the strain of the slope.

Al’s heart rate is now up to 150 beats per minute, and Ed’s is hitting almost 130.

Watching anxiously from Earth, Fred asks them to take a break.

“OK. We’re really going up a pretty steep slope here,” reports Ed.

“Yeah. We kind of figured that from listening to you,” says Fred.

Al takes another look up to what he thinks is the rim of Cone Crater. They’re almost two hours into their walk and Al estimates it will probably take them another 30 minutes to get there.

Ed agrees. “What we were looking at was a flank. It wasn’t the rim of Cone. We’ve got a ways to go yet.”
“We’re approaching the edge of the boulder field here on the south flank,” reports Al. “And what I’m proposing is perhaps we use that as the turnaround point.”

Al figures that stopping just up ahead, rather than pressing on for another half an hour, will mean they can spend more time collecting samples and taking photos. But it means they won’t get to set eyes on the view they’ve both dreamed of seeing for so long.

Ed can’t believe what Al’s suggesting. The edge of Cone Crater is the summit he’s been training to reach for so long – he can’t imagine turning back before he gets there.

“Huh?” he says, questioning Al’s proposal.

“I don’t think we’ll have time to go up there,” Al repeats.
“Oh, let’s give it a whirl,” says Ed encouragingly. “Gee whiz. We can’t stop without looking into Cone Crater.”
“I think we’ll waste an awful lot of time travelling and not much documenting,” says Al.
“Well, the information we’re going to find, I think, is going to be right on top,” replies Ed, searching for reasons to keep going.

Ed is right. From experiments done on Earth, it’s clear that the closer you get to the edge of an impact crater, the greater the depth from which the excavated material on the ground has come.

“Fredo, how far behind our timeline are we?” Ed asks, hoping to win the argument for carrying on to the edge of the crater.

Fred does a quick calculation. “OK. As best I can tell right now, you’re now about 25 minutes down.”

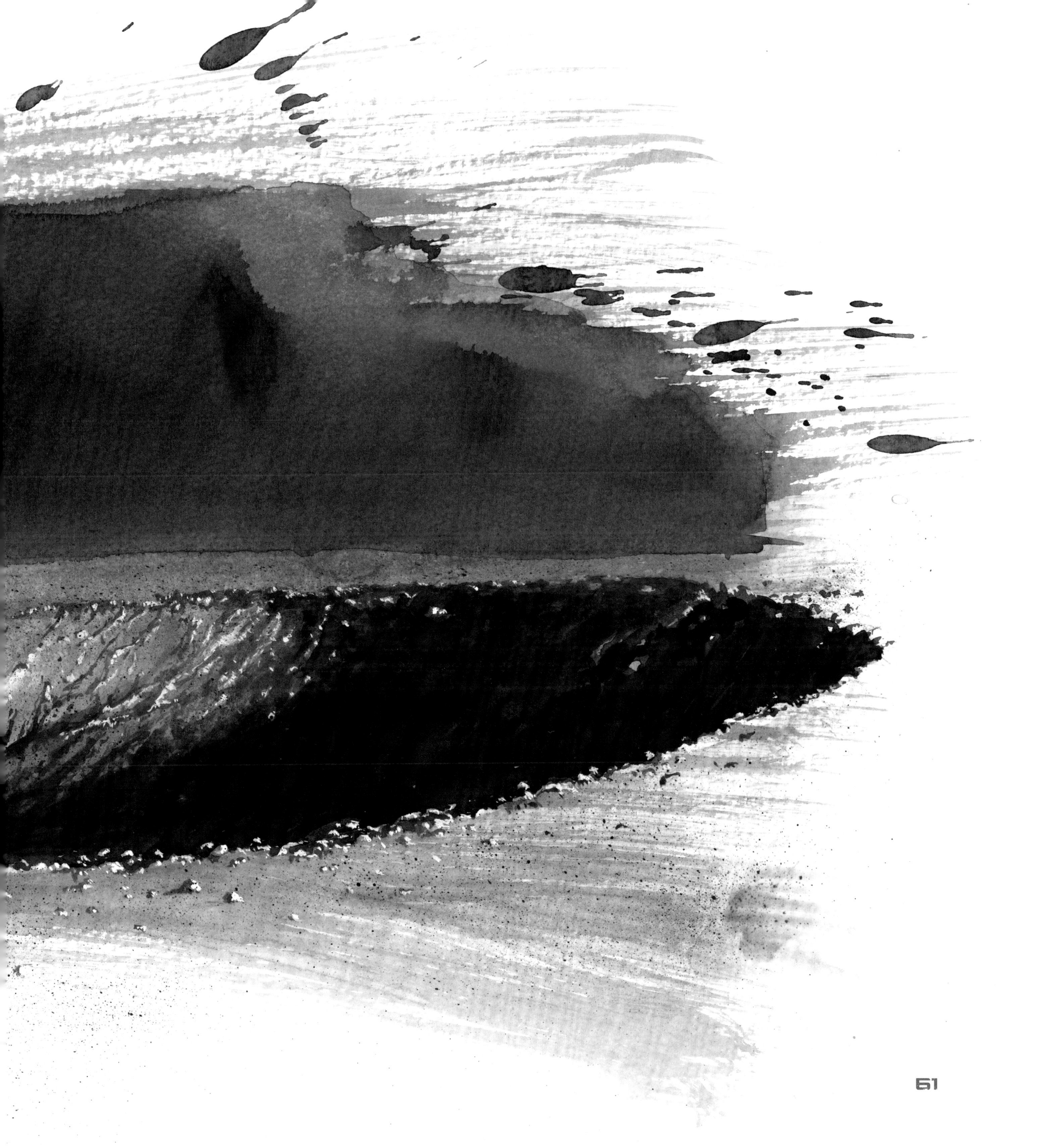

"OK," replies Ed, sensing that his chances of making it to Cone Crater are slipping away.

"We'll be an hour down by the time we get to the top of that thing," points out Al. "You got six samples," he continues, pointing out how few rocks they've collected so far.

"Well, I think we're going to find what we're looking for up there," repeats Ed, in desperation.
"OK, Al and Ed," chips in Fred, trying to stop the argument that's breaking out on the Moon. "In view of your assay [rock collection] and of where your location is and how long it's going to take to get to Cone, the word from the Backroom is they'd like you to consider where you are [now] the edge of Cone Crater."

Ed is fuming. "Think you're finks!" he calls out, exasperated by Fred's decision to side with Al, and accusing them both of being spoilsports.

"That decision, I guess, was based on Al's estimate of another, at least, 30 minutes and, of course, we cannot see that from here. It's kind of your judgment on that," says Fred, trying to make Ed feel better.
"Well, we're three-quarters there," replies Ed. "Why don't we leave the MET and get on up there? We could make it a lot faster without it," he says, still fighting for his chance to reach Cone Crater.
"Well... I think what we're looking at right here in this boulder field, Ed, is the stuff that's ejected from Cone," argues Al.
"But not the lowermost part, which is what we're interested in," retorts Ed.
"OK. We'll press on a little farther, Houston. And keep an eye on the time," concedes Al.
"OK. And, as of right now, we have a 30-minute extension," responds Fred. "Al, did you copy 30-minute extension?" he repeats.
"We got it," says Ed gratefully.
"Yeah. That's affirmative, Fred. Thank you," responds Al.

"Well, I'll tell you, it's a fantastic view from here," continues Al, breathing heavily again. "We're approaching the edge of the rugged boulder field to the west rim."

They press on, still hauling the MET, in the hope that they haven't got much further to go.

Four minutes later, to their relief, the ground starts to flatten out again.
"OK. We're about the maximum elevation now, Houston," reports Al. "It's levelled out a little bit. And it looks like we'll be approaching the rim here very shortly."

They take another break to discuss their position and describe the boulder field they're standing in.
"Al and Ed, do you have the rim in sight at this time?" asks Fred.
"Oh, yeah," says Ed, thinking Fred asked about the LEM and not the rim.
"It's affirmative. It's down in the valley," replies Al, also thinking Fred asked if they could still see their spaceship over a mile away.
"I'm sorry. You misunderstood the question. I meant the rim of Cone Crater," says Fred, correcting them.
"Oh, the rim. That is negative. We haven't found that yet," replies Al, sounding despondent.

Ed is disheartened too. He'd really thought that the crater edge would be there in front of them as they came up that last ridge and the ground flattened out. But it's nowhere to be seen. Although he's sure they are close, Ed's resigned to the fact he just doesn't know where they really are. Reluctantly, he's also beginning to think it's probably time to give up and head back.

"Ed and Al, we've already eaten in our 30-minute extension and we're past that now," says Fred. "I think we'd better proceed with the sampling and continue with the EVA."

"OK," replies Ed, accepting the wisdom of making this their furthest point. Doing so will allow them to travel slowly back to the spacecraft, sampling more as they go, rather than spending the time trying to reach the crater and then just racing straight back without stopping. It makes sense in terms of the science, but privately he finds the disappointment of realising he will never get to look into the gigantic Cone Crater heartbreaking.

It's something Ed will regret for the rest of his life.*

Back at their spaceship around an hour and a half later, and now in front of the camera again, Ed and Al are packing up to leave when Al surprises everyone. Hidden in a pocket strapped to his left leg is the metal head of a golf club. Al pulls it out and screws it on to the end of a long handled tool he's carrying, turning it into an improvised golf club.

To everyone's further surprise, he then pulls out a golf ball, drops it on to the Moon and prepares to take a swing at it.

"Unfortunately, the suit is so stiff, I can't do this with two hands…" he declares, making excuses for what might be a very poor attempt to hit the ball with the world watching, "…but I'm going to try a little sand-trap shot here."

Al takes his best one-armed swing at the ball, missing it almost completely.
"You got more dirt than ball that time," chuckles Ed.
"Got more dirt than ball," echoes Al. "Here we go again."
Al's second swing knocks the ball about a metre forwards, towards the camera.

"That looked like a slice to me, Al," jokes Fred, enjoying the chance to make fun of his friend. Undeterred, Al steps forward to take a third swing at the ball.
"Here we go. Straight as a die!" he predicts. "One more."
Al's final attempt is not much better than the last one.

* Six weeks after getting back to Earth, a careful analysis of their attempt to walk to Cone Crater reveals that they got within 100 metres of the summit. Had they walked just another six or seven metres further they'd have realised that.

"Miles and miles and miles," he crows, attempting to disguise his poor performance!
"Very good, Al," smiles Fred, amused by the whole pantomime.

Not wanting to be outdone for attempting a sporting first on the Moon, a few minutes later Ed has dismantled the Solar Wind Collector flag experiment, like the one Buzz put up during the first moonwalk, and removed the main flagpole. He walks towards the TV camera and assumes the position of a javelin thrower, with the pole held above his head in one hand.

Al is watching. "There's the greatest javelin throw of the century!" he announces.
"We'll see if it is," cries Ed, lunging forward and hurling the staff as hard as he can into the black sky. The pole doesn't travel far – coming to rest in the dirt, just past the golf ball.
"Outstanding! Right in the middle of the crater," comments Al.
"Stayed up," boasts Ed.
"Stabilised spin!" praises Al.
"Wasn't bad at all," admits Ed.
"Beautiful. Beautiful!" beams Al.

HADLEY RILLE
SATURDAY JULY 31ST 1971

ON THE SURFACE OF THE MOON
DAVE SCOTT CDR
(COMMANDER)
JIM IRWIN LMP
(LUNAR MODULE PILOT)

VOICE FROM EARTH
JOE ALLEN CAPCOM (CAPSULE COMMUNICATOR)

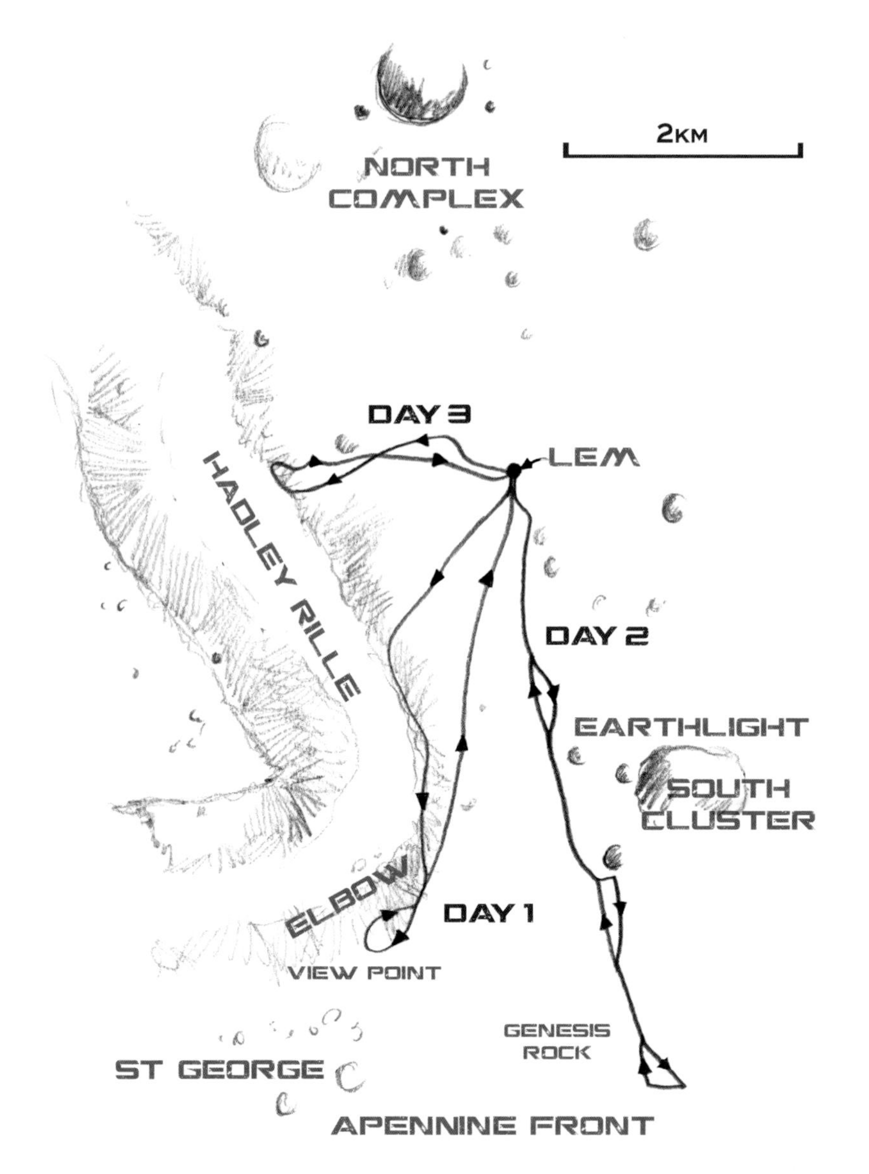

APOLLO 15 LANDING SITE MAP

1:29PM

"Man must explore," declares Dave, "and this is exploration at its greatest," he adds, stepping on to the Moon. He's standing over 1000 kilometres north of Cone Crater, where Al and Ed walked less than six months ago. In fact, he and his pal Jim are further north than anyone's ever stood on the Moon, at a place called Hadley Rille.

The word 'rille' (pronounced ry-ll) refers to the long winding canyon that cuts through the valley they've landed in. It's about 130 kilometres long and looks a bit like a winding river valley. But this canyon was not carved by water. It was formed by lava flowing beneath the Moon's surface, carving out a tube, millions of years ago. Since then the roof of this gigantic tube has collapsed, creating a deep gorge known as a 'rille'. Close to where Dave and Jim have landed, it's over 370 metres deep – enough to swallow the Eiffel Tower!

Hadley Rille cuts through a rugged region known as the Apennine Mountains. They're the first mountains on the Moon that anyone's ever visited. And they are BIG, rising five kilometres out of the surrounding plains. Some peaks are taller than the mighty Himalayan Mountains on Earth. Dominating their view to the northeast is one truly enormous peak known as Mount Hadley. It towers imposingly 4200 metres above Dave, and made landing here tricky. To avoid hitting it, Dave and Jim had to make the steepest descent ever attempted on a Moon landing. But their trailblazing flight path has brought them to a very special valley.

Geologists think the mountains around them were formed from ancient moon rock pushed upwards by one of the largest impacts ever to happen in the entire solar system. This gigantic collision occurred almost four billion years ago, when an object maybe 250 kilometres across hit the Moon somewhere near here. This crash cracked the Moon's crust open and molten lava flooded out, covering a immense area the size of western Europe. As it cooled, this vast expanse of darker lava formed the left eye of the face we see on the Moon from Earth today.

Excitingly, this means that the mountains Dave is now marvelling at around him are made of the original moon rock that was here before this gigantic impact. And that makes them very old indeed; older than most rocks on Earth. It's Dave's dream to try to bring a piece back for the geologists to study.

The other reason they've landed here is to visit a cluster of craters to the south – thought to have been formed from debris hurled here from another more recent impact 160 kilometres to the north. Collecting these rocks will allow them to gather samples from somewhere far away without having to go there. But visiting all these locations will still mean them travelling further than anyone's ever travelled before on the Moon.

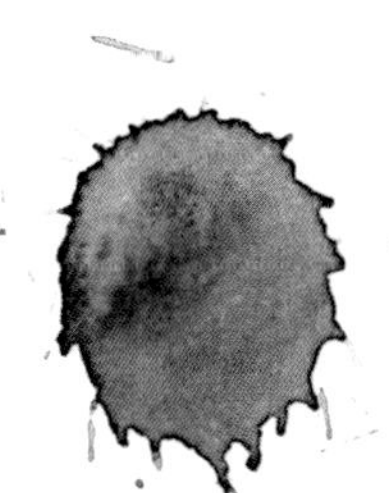

To help them get around, Dave and Jim have brought an electric car. The roving vehicle or 'rover' for short is currently folded up beneath their spacecraft, and their first job will be to unpack and assemble it. But first Dave needs to check it hasn't been damaged on the way here.

"Well, I see why we're in a tilt," he observes, stepping back from *Falcon* – the name they've chosen for their spaceship. From where he's standing, he can see it's slipped downslope in the soft dirt, tipping back and raising the pad at the foot of their ladder slightly off the ground. "But the LEM looks like it's in good shape. And the rover's in good shape," he adds.

Dave's itching to start unpacking the rover, but before he can begin he needs to get his pal Jim out of the spacecraft. Their hatch has not opened fully for some reason and Jim is struggling to exit.

"Hey, Dave, can you tell what I'm hung up on here?" asks Jim.
"OK, let me come over. Just a second. Stay right there," replies Dave.

He hops back up a rung or two on the ladder to get a better look. Jim has had to move to his right to work around the half-open hatch and Dave can see he's caught his right side on the opening.

"OK, come left, Jim," he instructs. "OK, now ease back out. Head down."

Jim manages to squeeze through the narrowed hatchway and backs out further.

"Keep coming. Ease out. That a boy," instructs Dave encouragingly. "OK, you're clear."
"OK. I'm closing the hatch," replies Jim as he starts down the ladder.
"Oh, and it's dirty out here," warns Dave, hopping back on to the Moon.

Jim follows quickly behind him, taking his first step into the dust. "Your boots are black already," he says to Dave, looking down at them.
"And so are yours," retorts Dave.

"Oh, boy. It's beautiful out here!" says Jim looking up at the dramatic view. "Reminds me of Sun Valley," he continues, recalling a ski resort in North America.

"Roger Jim," says a man called Joe Allen, their friendly assistant listening in back on Earth.

"No wonder we slid, Dave," says Jim, stepping into a deeper patch of dust. "Boy, that's really soft dirt there around the front footpad."
"Sure is, isn't it?" replies Dave.
"Like about six inches deep of soft material," says Jim.
"That's also like Sun Valley, Jim," says Joe.
"Yeah, powder," replies Jim, remembering the snow at the resort.

"OK, Jim. Let's take a look at our rover friend here," says Dave, keen to get going. He heads over to the right side of the rover. "OK, the outriggers look OK," he says, relieved that it's not suffered any visible damage from the landing.

"OK, I'm going to go up the platform," says Jim, about to climb up to the porch where he will pull a long strap, known as a lanyard, that will start the rover's release from the spacecraft.
"OK. Don't pull it yet," warns Dave.

Jim grabs the ladder with both hands and leaps up on to it, using his arms and legs to scramble towards the porch with ease. He seems to almost float in the lower gravity here on the Moon. Both men are very fit, and they delight in the feeling of being as strong as they would be on Earth while weighing just a sixth of their Earth weight. It feels like they have superpowers.

While Jim swings with ease up the outside of the spacecraft, Dave keeps up his visual inspection of the rover. Other than a couple of hinges that seem to have come loose on the way, the vehicle looks to be in good condition.
"Whenever you're ready," says Jim, standing by.
"OK, Jim, go ahead," replies Dave.
"OK, here it comes," calls Jim, tugging on the lanyard. The top of the rover tips forwards, pivoting on a pair of hinges below.

"Released," cries Jim, climbing back down.

"OK. Ready? Here we go," says Dave.
Jim grabs the lanyard in one hand and backs away, pulling the folded up rover out further towards them. In his other hand he's holding a camera and trying to photograph their progress.

"Oh! Oh! That a boy," calls out Dave reassuringly. "A little more. Little more."
Jim backs further away, keeping the lanyard taut. "Looks like you're going to have to do the bulk of the work today," jokes Dave. "More. Keep it taut. Atta boy. Easy, Jim! Easy!"

Jim continues backing away as the rover drops down further. Just as the rear wheels spring out and lock into position, Jim steps back into a particularly soft patch of dirt and topples over backwards, sending moon dust flying around him.

"Oops!" exclaims Dave as he spots Jim lying on his back. Both men burst out laughing.
"Here, let me help you," calls Dave, reaching out his arm to pull Jim up again.

Back on his feet, Jim continues to tug on the lanyard. "Take it easy, take it easy," Dave continues, coaxing the rover out on to the Moon. "OK, come on up. Up we go! Come on. Easy!"

Jim tugs a little more and the rear chassis of the rover clicks into place as the entire car swings out from the spacecraft revealing the main driving controls. With a bit more of a pull, the front wheels lock into place, and the whole vehicle pops out backwards on to the Moon.

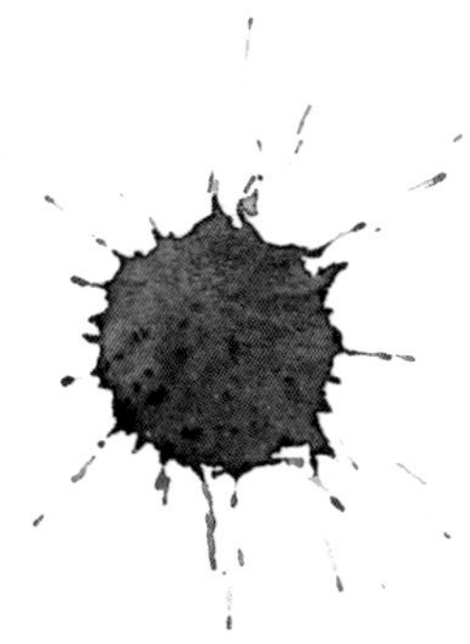

"How's that?" asks Jim.
"That looks good," says Dave, pleased with their progress. He steps forward and grabs hold of the centre of the vehicle's chassis, gently lifting it.
"Man, this thing's nice and light," he comments, surprised by how little effort it takes to raise the entire vehicle off the Moon.
Both men lift again, in an attempt to disconnect it from the *Falcon* spacecraft.
"OK, Joe, it's off," reports Jim.
"Outstanding," replies Joe.

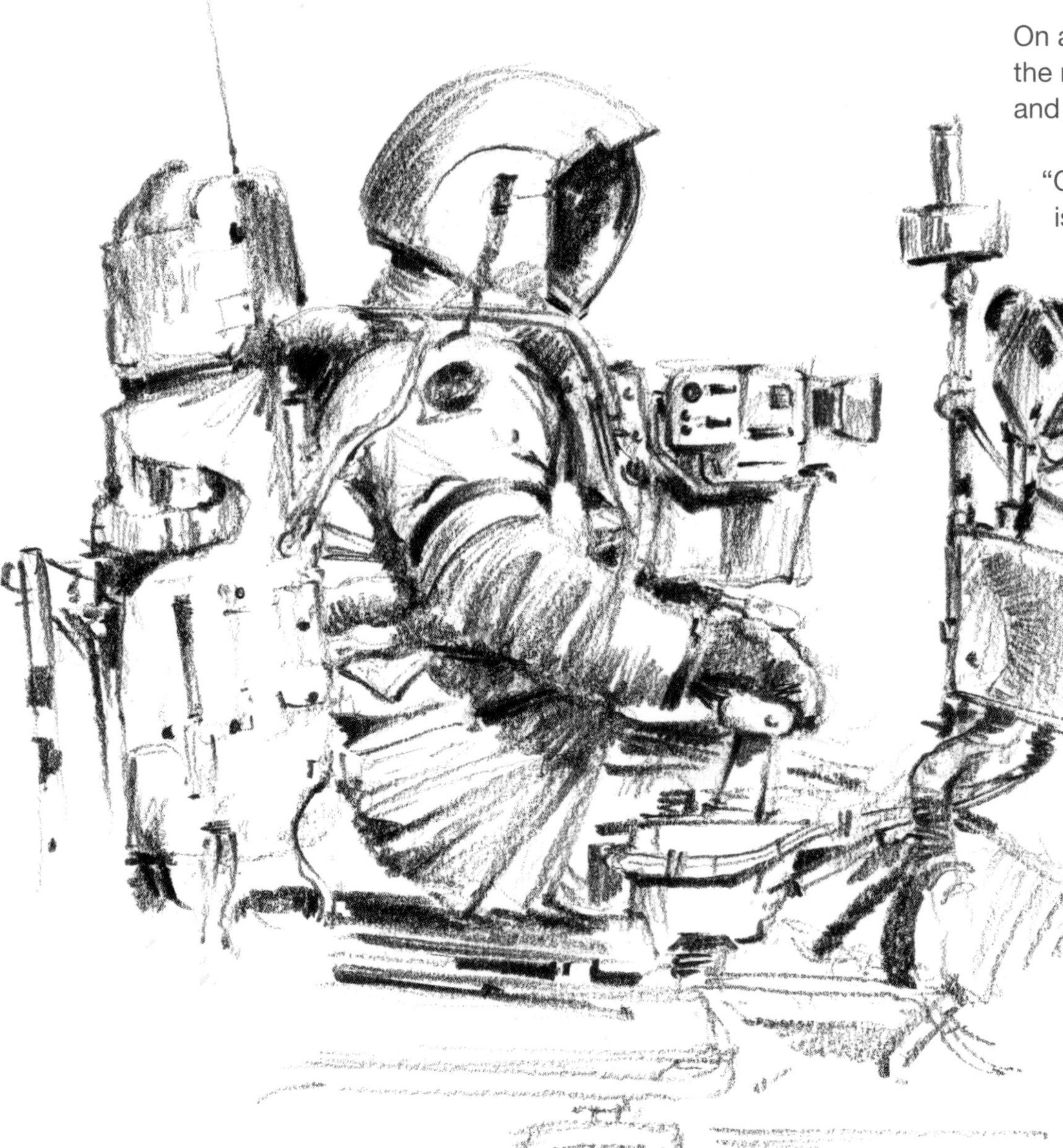

Jim and Dave lift the car once more and carry it out a little way from the spacecraft to set it up. The seats are strapped flat with strips of Velcro to make it easier for the astronauts to undo them with their gloves. Once in position, they work to release the rover's seat belts, and then start unfurling the wheel guards – or fenders as they call them. These orange covers are designed to stop the rover kicking up too much dust.

"OK, looks like the brake's on, so I'll see if I can't hop in it," says Dave, leaping on to the left seat. "That's a reasonable fit."
"OK, Dave," acknowledges Joe. "And buckle up for safety here," he adds.
"Oh, yeah," replies Dave, reaching for his belt.

On a drive across the undulating lunar surface there's the real possibility of him or Jim falling off the rover, and so the seat belts are crucial.

"OK, hand controller is locked. Brake's on, reverse is down," says Dave, working through his checklist. Dave's one of the best pilots of his generation – and a master of the checklist. He's flown some of the fastest machines in the world, including three different spacecraft, and while this is probably the slowest craft he's ever taken the controls of, he's leaving nothing to chance.

The rover's four wheels are each driven by their own electric motor, giving the vehicle great power to cope with steep slopes and deep dust. What's more, the car's front and rear wheels can also steer – making it highly manoeuvrable.

"OK," says Dave taking the rover out of its park mode. "Out of detent; we're moving."
"Extraordinary!" exclaims Joe, as incredulous as Dave and Jim that they're now actually DRIVING on the Moon!

"Hey, Jim, you can probably tell me if I've got any rear steering?" asks Dave.

"Yeah, you have rear steering," replies Jim.
"But I don't have any front steering," reports Dave.
"Got just rear steering, Dave," Jim confirms.

Back on Earth, Joe confers with his colleagues and quickly recommends adjusting the battery power to divert it to the front wheel steering. It doesn't work. But Dave is prepared for this event and has practised driving on Earth with only front or rear steering. The important thing is that they are motoring – and it's time to explore!

"Boy, we're going to have a great time with all these hills and mounds," Dave says, thrilled at the prospect of becoming the first person to go off-roading off-Earth!

Dave circles the rover back towards Jim and they start to load it up for their first excursion. They transfer the TV camera on to it, connecting it to a mobile satellite dish on the front of the vehicle, so Joe and the rest of the world can receive pictures from each location they visit.

"Let's do a little geology," calls out Joe, urging them to get going.

"That a boy!" replies Dave – eager to get to work. Although an accomplished military test pilot and astronaut, Dave has also been studying the geology of the Moon for years, and he's eager to put his knowledge of our neighbouring world to the test now he's here.

Dave jumps back on to the left seat and Jim hops on to the right. The rover rocks violently.

"Hey. This thing's really bouncy when you get on," cries Dave in surprise. "Easy, easy, easy, Jim. Easy."

Without the gravity of Earth pulling them into their seats more firmly and compressing their pressurised suits, both men feel more like they're sitting on the car rather than in it.
"You really sit high," says Jim, surprised by their position.
"Yes, you do," agrees Dave.
"It's almost like standing up," notes Jim.

After adjusting their seat belts again for their raised positions, they prepare to set off.
"OK, Jim, here we go," announces Dave, nudging the central controller stick forwards.

The moon car is not steered with a steering wheel, but with something more like the control stick of an aircraft. It's in the centre of the rover between the two seats, meaning that either astronaut can drive; although in practice it is always the man in the left seat, the commander of the mission, who will take control.*

"OK, Dave. We want a heading of 203," notes Jim, setting their course for the first destination.
"OK, 203," acknowledges Dave.

After Ed and Al's difficulty navigating just one kilometre from their spacecraft, the rover's designers have been careful to build a more effective navigation system for Dave and Jim; one that won't require them to constantly stop and work out where they are on the map.

It works by setting everything to zero before they set off from the spacecraft each day. It then records the number of turns of each wheel to measure the distance driven. Changes in the rover's direction are recorded by a spinning gyroscope inside a box at the front of the vehicle. It works in the same way as a toy gyroscope, which resists attempts to change its orientation; so each time the rover is steered in a different direction, it creates a force that is measured. Together these details of the journey are fed into a simple onboard computer that does some mathematical calculations, known as trigonometry, to keep a record of where they are.

Dave will drive while Jim keeps an eye on the navigation console and a lookout for interesting geology to investigate.
"OK, we're moving forward, Joe," reports Jim for the benefit of those listening on Earth.

* The stick is more of a T-shaped handle that the astronaut rests their palm on top of – pushing it gently forward to go forward, left to steer left and right to steer right. Bringing it back into the centre position will stop the vehicle, and flipping a switch with your thumb and then pulling it backwards will put the rover into reverse. The parking brake is applied by pulling the T-handle back further than 15°.

"Roger," replies Joe.

"Whew! Hang on," says Dave, as he adjusts to how the rover, now fully laden, is handling.
"We're coming around left," reports Jim. "Heading directly south right now to miss some craters off to our right – very subdued craters."
"OK, I'm going to take a little zigzag here..." says Dave, pushing the stick left and right to dodge the craters.
"OK, we're doing ten kilometres now," reports Jim.
Dave points the rover up a gentle slope and accelerates again, exhilarated by the ride.
"No dust, Joe, no dust at all," he notes in surprise, delighted that the predictions they'd be covered in dust thrown up by their rover's wire wheels have not come to pass.

The terrain undulates repeatedly – making the drive feel like more of a boat ride across a choppy sea.

"Boy, it's really rolling hills, Joe. Just like 14," Dave continues, referring to Al and Ed's trek to Cone Crater.
"Up and down we go," he cries as they hit the crest of another rise.

Dave continues to manoeuvre around the craters and depressions, using the rover's rear wheel steering to navigate the hummocky terrain.
"OK Joe, the rover handles quite well," he reports.
"It negotiates small craters quite well, although there's a lot of roll. It feels like we need the seat belts, doesn't it, Jim?"
"Yeah, really do," Jim agrees.
Dave swerves again to avoid another small crater.
"Whoa! Hang on," he warns, his eyes fixed ahead.
"How we doing on the heading, Jimmer?"
"OK," reports Jim, "if we're heading right for Elbow..." referring to a crater near a sharp bend in the Rille ahead.

The rover hits another mound and leaps off the ground.
"Boy, it really bounces, doesn't it?" cries Jim, hanging on for dear life.
"Man, this is really a rocking-rolling ride, isn't it?" chuckles Dave.
"Never been on a ride like this before," agrees Jim.
"Hey, you can see the Rille!" shouts Jim. "There's the Rille."
"There's the Rille," repeats Dave, glancing up at the giant valley that unfolds before them.
"Yeah. We're looking down and across the Rille," notes Jim, "we can see craters on the far side."
"Yes, sir. We're on the edge of the Rille, you'd better believe it," confirms Dave.
"Oh, yeah, I see Elbow," Jim reports.
"Oh, there's some beautiful geology out here," says Dave. "Spectacular!"

Distracted by the view, Dave hits a small crater that was hidden by a rise.
"Oops! Watch out. Hold on," he warns. The rover takes off again briefly – landing gracefully half a metre further on. "Whew, whoopee!" he cries enjoying the thrill of the ride.
"You'd better watch the road, Dave," says Jim.

As Dave continues driving along the edge of the Rille, Joe is interested to check on the rover's performance.
"Dave, are the front wheels wandering off of straight ahead as you drive along there?" he asks.
"No, they're OK, Joe," replies Dave. "It's just… there are a lot of craters and it's just sporty driving; I've just got to keep my eye on the road every second."
"Roger. We understand that..." replies Joe.
Jim is still hanging on tightly as Dave continues swerving around every crater and boulder coming their way.
"This is really a sporty driving course," he declares.
"Man, oh man, what a Grand Prix this is!"

Dave's sporty driving has bought them some extra time and they stop at Elbow crater to take some samples and photographs before pressing on.

"OK. We're on the way," Dave reports. "Oh, boy! This is travelling! This is a great sport, I'll tell you."

"Jim, as you look back, can you see the rover tracks?" asks Joe.
"Oh, standby..." says Jim, craning backwards to take a look.
"Yeah, we could, Joe," chips in Dave. "I saw them when we stopped at the last stop."
"OK, good," notes Joe, pleased that if they get lost they can always follow their tracks back to the *Falcon*. "Sounds like the old Hansel and Gretel trick'll work," he smiles.

Dave drives steadily uphill for a few more minutes to reach their next stop on the edge of the southern mountain. The rover has carried them higher than they've been so far, right above the floor of the valley their spaceship landed in. It's an unforgettable view.

"Oh, look back there, Jim!" exclaims Dave. "Look at that. Oh, look at that! Isn't that something? We're up on a slope, Joe, and we're looking back down into the valley and..."

"That's beautiful," Jim jumps in.

"That is spectacular!" continues Dave. "Man, you all ought to have a great view this time. OK, Jim; let's go sample this rock."

The two of them climb off the rover and set about collecting rocks and taking panoramic photographs of the vista.

"The most beautiful thing I've ever seen," says Dave, his breath really taken away by the sight.

Dave walks a little higher towards one particular boulder that's caught his eye. It's particularly angular and has a rough texture. "Looks like it's got glass on one side of it," begins Dave, "with lots of bubbles; and they're about a centimetre across," he goes on.

It's clearly a very mixed up rock, a result of the violent history of the Moon, with regular impacts repeatedly breaking and fusing the rocks together.

"Roger, Dave and Jim..." says Joe, spellbound by Dave's description, and the view he's now got of them from the TV camera that's mounted on the front of the rover. "And it probably is fresh; probably..." he continues, "not older than three and a half billion years."

"Can you imagine that, Joe?" replies Dave, suddenly taken by the thought of such deep time. "Here sits this rock, and it's been here since before creatures roamed the sea in our little Earth."

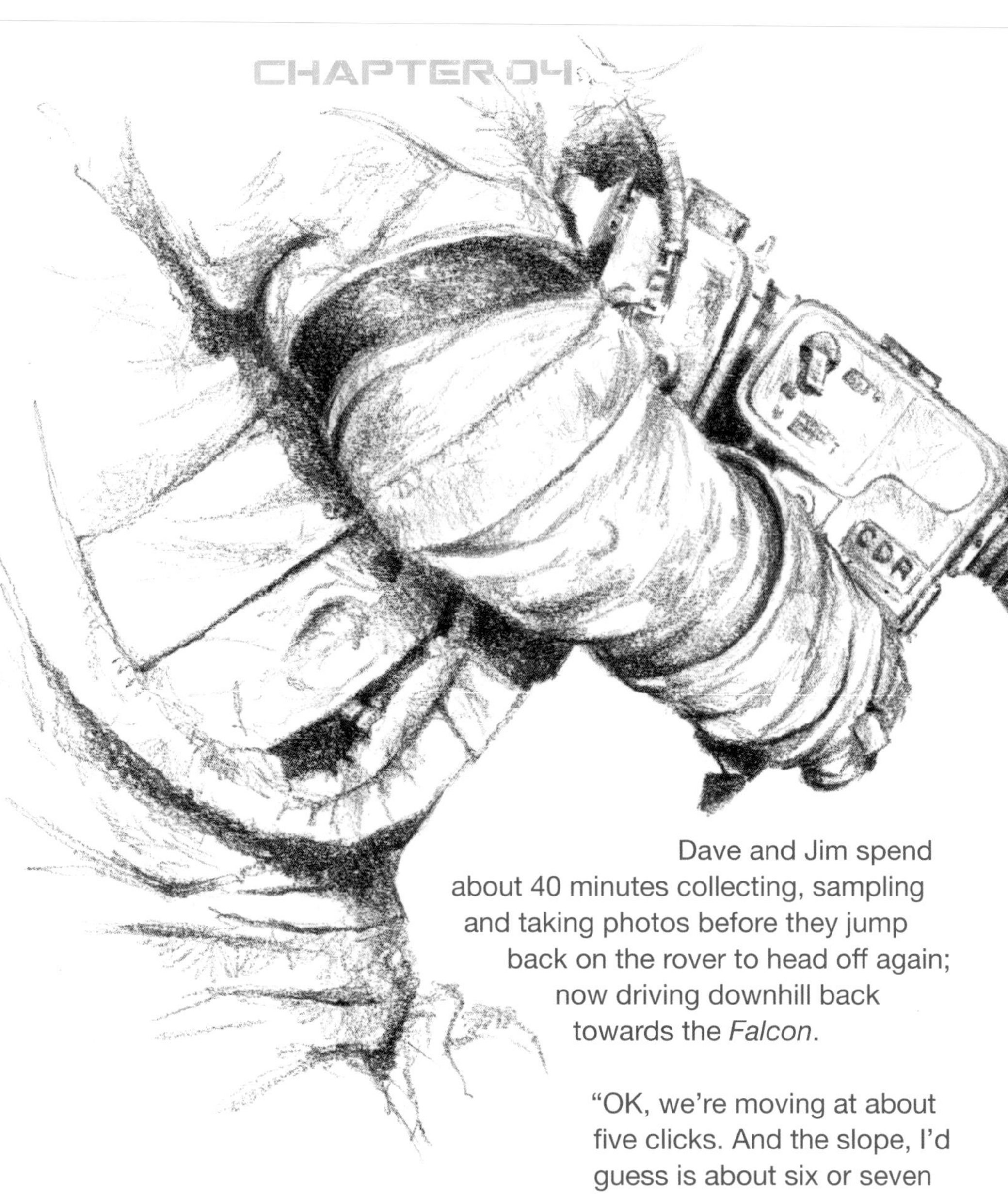

Dave and Jim spend about 40 minutes collecting, sampling and taking photos before they jump back on the rover to head off again; now driving downhill back towards the *Falcon*.

"OK, we're moving at about five clicks. And the slope, I'd guess is about six or seven degrees; and we're going cross-slope," notes Jim, as they traverse the sloping ground.
"Any idea of whether you can see the LEM or not?" asks Joe, curious to know if they can spot the *Falcon* out there in the distance.
"Well Joe, I took a look when we were up there and I couldn't see it," replies Dave.
Dave and Jim are the first astronauts ever to lose sight of their spaceship, and now they're relying on the rover's navigation system to help them find it again.

Dave points the rover straight downslope and does his best to avoid the craters.
"Whooee!" he cries, enjoying the lively off-road driving.
"I didn't realise we'd gone up so high," says Jim, clinging on as Dave speeds downhill, zig-zagging around depressions and rocks.
Suddenly the rover's front wheels dig into the soft dust.
"Hang on. Whoa! Hang on!" cries Dave as the vehicle spins around 180 degrees, bouncing to a halt facing abruptly uphill in the opposite direction.
Both men start laughing, relieved that they didn't flip over.
"Got to go easy downhill, huh?" says Dave, slightly embarrassed that he's spun the car.
"I'd say so," giggles Jim, just pleased to have survived!
"What a ride!" chuckles Dave, setting off again.

The slope levels off as they drop back towards the valley floor.
"Yeah, man. There are some rover tracks!" calls out Dave, noticing their outbound wheel marks heading towards them. "How about that?"
"Yeah, somebody else has been here," jokes Jim, pleased that the rover's navigation system seems to be guiding them back.
Over the next rise something catches his eye, gleaming in the sunlight.
"I think that's the LEM," he calls out, spying their beloved *Falcon* in the distance.
"Yeah. Yeah," agrees Dave.
"Yeah, we see it, Joe," confirms Jim.
"Sure do. And we're heading right straight for it," says Dave. "Boy, I'll tell you, Joe, this is a super way to travel; nice and cool; uphill without any strain. This is great," he continues in sheer delight with how the very first drive on the Moon has gone.
"There's home," cries Jim – relieved to be returning to the relative safety of their spacecraft.

After a nap and a bunch of chores to maintain the *Falcon*, the pair set off on their second drive. Their route will take them south again towards the cluster of craters the geologists think were created from debris hurled from an impact over 100 kilometres north of here.

Before they set off, Joe wants them to try to reset the front steering again. Dave is hopeful that it might work, and wants to share a little joke with Joe.

"You know what I bet you did last night, Joe?" he says. "You let some of those Marshall guys come up here and fix it, didn't you?"
Marshall is one of the engineering centres in America where the rover was developed.
"They've been working. That's for sure," replies Joe, aware that a crack team of rover engineers has been up all night trying to figure out a solution for Dave and Jim to try this morning.

Dave resets the switches that Joe recommends and nudges the control stick forward, attempting to steer. To their delight it works. Jim laughs with joy.
"It works, Dave!" he shouts, hardly believing their luck.
"Yes, sir. It's working, my friend," replies Dave – also pleased with the rover's renewed capabilities.
"Beautiful," cheers Jim.
"Lot of smiles on that one, Dave," replies Joe, looking around him at his grinning colleagues in the control room.

Over the three days that Dave and Jim spend on the Moon, their trusty rover – LRV-1 – will carry them a total of 27.9 kilometres; more than ten times further than Ed and Al managed to cover on foot. It helps them collect 78 kilograms of moon rocks – more than twice as much as the previous mission. Among these rocks is Sample Number *15415*. This small, precious, speckled white rock is made of lots of beautiful crystals that formed about four thousand million years ago, when the Moon and the Earth were both very young, and long before any life had got started. Those watching from Earth name it the Genesis Rock. It's just what Dave dreamed of finding.

Back at the spaceship for the last time, there's one final trick Dave's been planning.
"Joe, I hope you have a good picture there," he says.
"Beautiful picture there, Dave," replies Joe, excited by what's to come.

Dave is standing facing the camera. He's holding a couple of objects.
"In my left hand, I have a feather; in my right hand, a hammer," he exclaims. "And I guess one of the reasons we got here today was because of a gentleman named Galileo, a long time ago, who made a rather significant discovery about falling objects in gravity fields. And we thought where would be a better place to confirm his findings than on the Moon."

Dave is referring to the Italian astronomer and mathematician Galileo Galilei, one of the first people to build a telescope out of glass lenses and point it to the sky. Galileo's breakthrough revealed that the Earth isn't at the centre of the Universe, but orbits the Sun instead. It was the beginning of a revolution in our understanding of the heavens that ultimately led to Dave standing on the Moon today – over 350 years later.

A man called Ed, who's controlling the TV camera from Earth, zooms in on the objects in Dave's hands to show everyone a clearer view of them. Dave is holding each out lightly, between his thumb and forefinger, ready for his demonstration.

"And so we thought we'd try it here for you," he continues. "The feather happens to be, appropriately, a falcon feather for our *Falcon*. And I'll drop the two of them here and, hopefully, they'll hit the ground at the same time."

Galileo had been the first to realise that all objects are subject to the same force of gravity, whatever their size and mass. On Earth, a feather only falls to the ground more slowly than a hammer because the air slows it down. But here on the Moon, without any air, Galileo's theory predicts that it will fall at the same rate as the hammer.

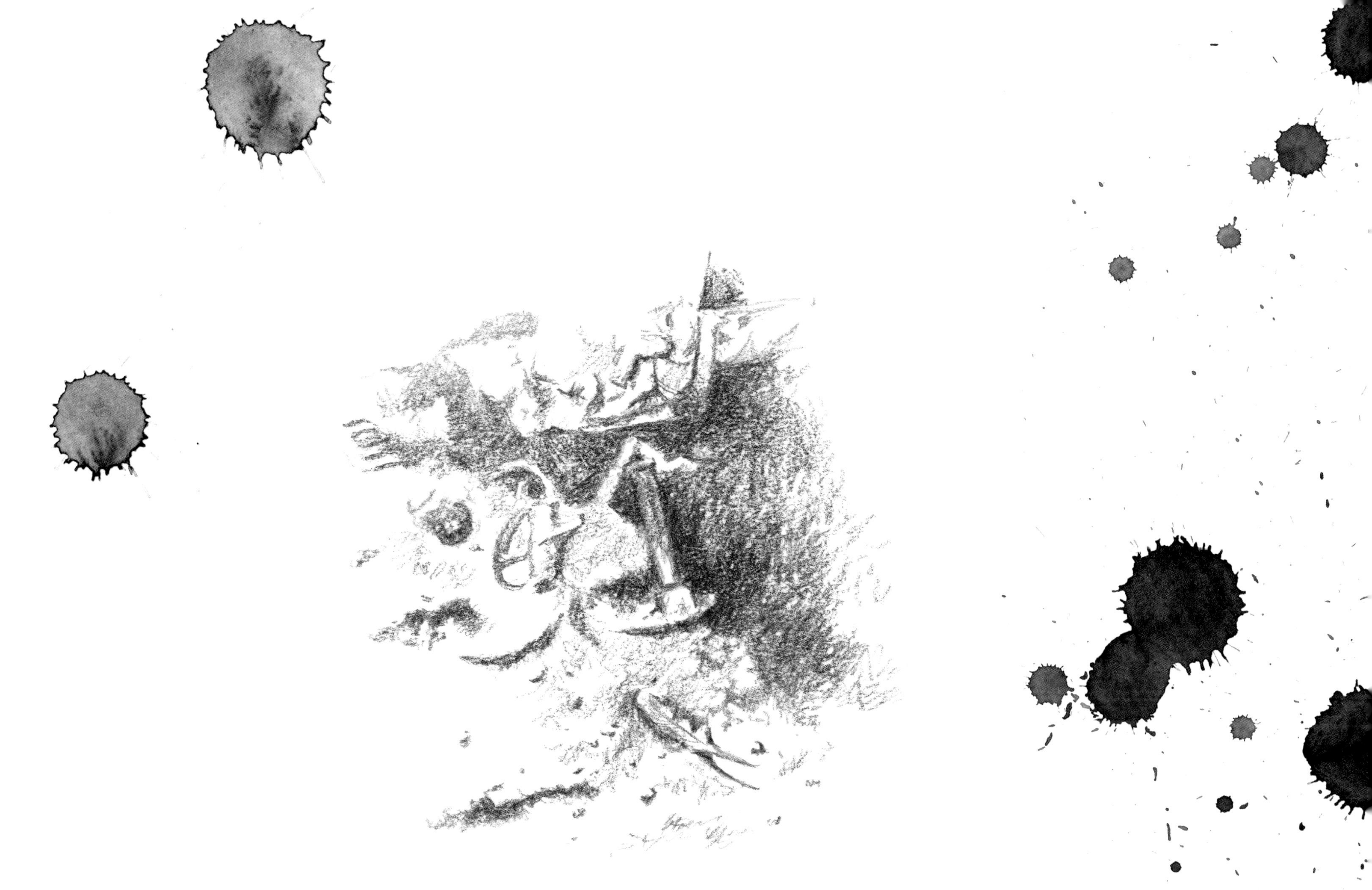

Ed zooms the camera out again to capture Dave releasing them together. The two objects drop in unison, hitting the ground together, just as Galileo had predicted.

"How about that!" he declares, delighted at the result and relieved he didn't screw up.*
"How about that!" repeats Joe – equally delighted. Everyone watching around him back on Earth starts to applaud.

* Dave had in fact carried two falcon feathers to the Moon to try a test before doing it on camera – in case any static electricity on the Moon stuck the feather to his glove or some other problem occurred. In the end he didn't have time for the practice – but luckily it went alright.

Dave continues his presentation. "Which proves that Mr Galileo was correct in his findings."
"Superb," replies Joe, still clapping. He and Dave came up with the idea before they left for the Moon and Joe's just thrilled at how it's gone.
"Nothing like a little science on the Moon, I always say," concludes Dave.

Before Dave and Jim can leave the Moon, Dave must drive the rover out to its final resting place and park it far enough away that the camera will have a view of them taking off.
Dave is heading for a slight rise above their landing site – about 90 metres away.
"OK, I think I've got a good place for you," he tells Joe. "I think you'll like this."

Once he's parked, Dave must reposition the dish antenna on the front of the rover to send the live TV pictures back to Earth. But he's having trouble locating his home planet.

"It's sure hard to see the Earth," he reports.
To accurately position the dish, Dave must use a kind of telescope, and it's not easy getting his eye to it from inside his helmet.

"Oh, Earth! Where are you? Can't get my visor…" he complains, straining to find it.
The Earth finally pops into view in the telescope and Dave locks on to it.
"OK, Joe, you should be aligned," he reports.
"OK, Dave, thank you," replies Joe, now picking up a picture from the rover camera.

While those back on Earth take control of the TV camera, Dave has one last thing he's been planning.

He takes a few more items out of his pockets. One of them, a small Bible with a red cover, he places gently up against the rover's console. Another is a little plaque with the names of the astronauts and cosmonauts who've lost their lives in the pursuit of space flight. Finally, there's a tiny metal statue of a space traveller – to symbolise these fallen star-men. He places these last two artefacts in the dust behind the rover.

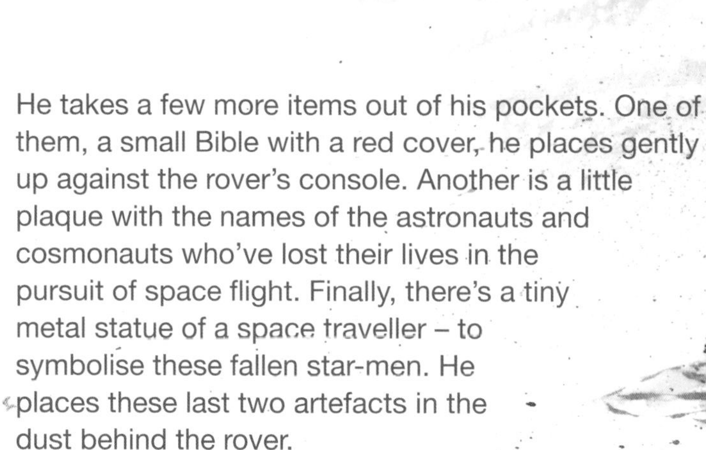

Dave takes a few steps back and snaps a series of photographs immortalising the resting place of humanity's first lunar rover vehicle. It will not be the last car to carry astronauts across the Moon.
Joe's voice intrudes into Dave's headset again, urging him to get a move on.
"We're interested in moving on back towards the LEM," he says.
"OK. Back to LEM,"
Dave acknowledges.

As Joe watches Dave trotting back towards the spaceship, to head home, he is reminded of a line from a character in one of his favorite science fiction stories, *The Green Hills of Earth* by a writer called Robert A. Heinlein. Joe starts to quote from it.
"As the space poet Rhysling would say, we're ready for you to come *'back again to the homes of men on the cool green hills of Earth.'*"

The Green Hills of Earth

Let the sweet fresh breezes heal me
As they rove around the girth
Of our lovely mother planet
Of the cool, green hills of Earth.

We've tried each spinning space mote
And reckoned its true worth:
Take us back again to the homes of men
On the cool, green hills of Earth.

The arching sky is calling
Spacemen back to their trade.
ALL HANDS! STAND BY! FREE FALLING!
And the lights below us fade.

Out ride the sons of Terra,
Far drives the thundering jet,
Up leaps a race of Earthmen,
Out, far, and onward yet ---

We pray for one last landing
On the globe that gave us birth;
Let us rest our eyes on the fleecy skies
And the cool, green hills of Earth.

Robert A. Heinlein, 1947

Descartes Highlands
Wednesday April 21st 1972

On the surface of the moon

John Young CDR
(Commander)

Charlie Duke LMP
(Lunar Module Pilot)

Voice from Earth

Tony England Capcom (Capsule Communicator)

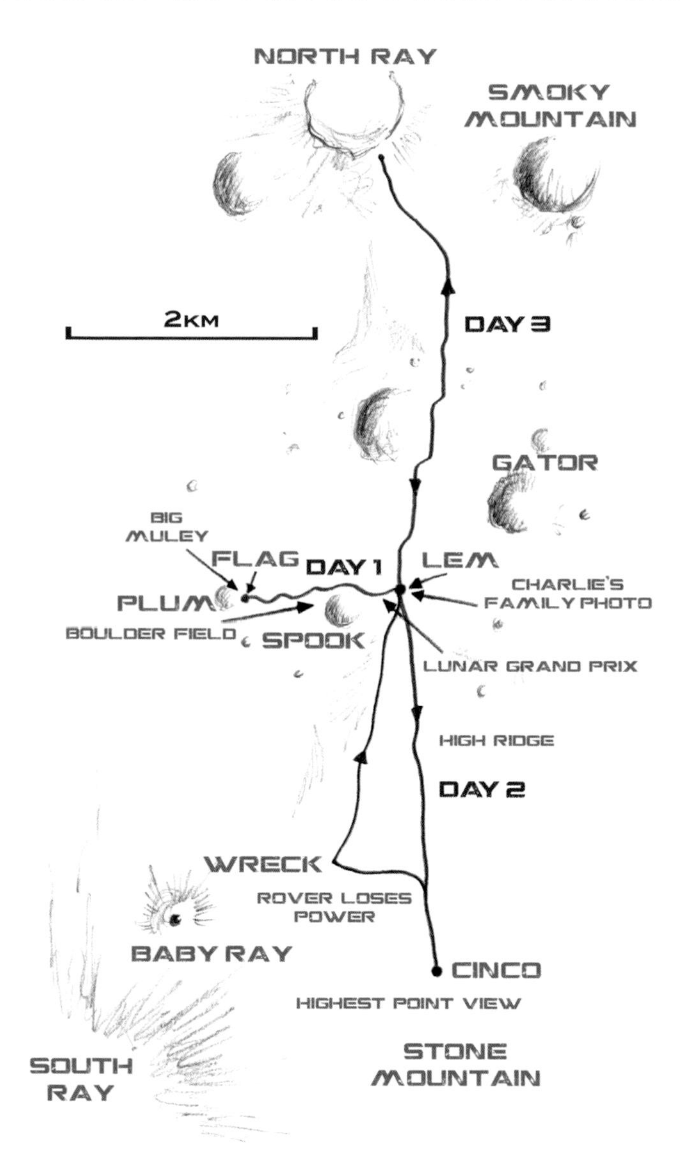

Apollo 16 landing site map

4:57PM

"I'm sure glad they got ol' Br'er Rabbit, here, back in the briar patch where he belongs," says John as he steps off his spacecraft on to the Moon. He's referring to an old children's story about a rabbit who felt at home in a patch of thorny bushes where most people would be miserable. And right now John is feeling at home, far from Earth, where most of us would feel uneasy.

John's made more flights into space than any other astronaut. This is his fourth mission. He's even been to the Moon once before, on a practise flight that paved the way for Neil and Buzz to make the very first landing. He didn't get to land then, but this time's different.

John and his friend Charlie have landed their spaceship *Orion* in a mountainous region known as the Descartes Highlands; a rugged landscape criss-crossed by ridges and slopes and covered in boulders. To the north the terrain rises into the rounded hills of Smoky Mountain. To the south lie the equally dramatic slopes of Stone Mountain. They will visit both peaks in the coming days.

John and Charlie are the ninth and tenth people in history to land on the Moon, and their arrival today has gone unnoticed by most of the other three billion people living back on Earth. But they don't mind.
For everyone who reaches the Moon, it is the pinnacle of their professional lives. Neither of them is here to be remembered. They are here for the thrill of the adventure. At 36 years old, Charlie is the youngest person to stand on the Moon. For years he's been working in teams helping his friends to get here, but today it's his turn and he can't wait to join John outside.

"Oh, is this ever neat, Charlie!" calls out John, revelling in the sensation of walking here.
"OK, I'm out. Almost," cries Charlie, nearly tumbling over himself to get out the door.
"Ho, ho. Is this ever nice..." continues John, dancing around.
Charlie leaps down the ladder. "Hot dog! Is this great!" he cheers.

"Sounds great," says Tony England – a young planetary scientist and trainee-astronaut who's listening from Earth.

Standing on the spacecraft's landing pad at the base of the ladder, Charlie peers under the spacecraft. He's so excited he can hardly get his words out.
"You can see the...This is easier than we..." he stutters, pausing to start again. "OK, John. You can see in the shadows just great!"

Charlie steps on to the Moon to join John.

"Fantastic!" he cries. "Oh, that first foot on the lunar surface is super, Tony!"
Charlie takes a second step.
"OK, Tony, we're making little footprints here about half an inch deep," he reports.

He and John have had a good sleep inside *Orion* here on the Moon before coming out to explore and it feels like he's woken up to his best birthday ever! Whether it's having spent years helping his friends get to the Moon, or all the training that he's done to get himself here, Charlie feels a strong sense of belonging. At times he's so comfortable he forgets where he is and even thinks about taking his helmet off. Without any air to breathe here on the Moon, he knows that this would be a bad idea, but he feels the urge all the same.

Back on Earth, athletes around the world are preparing to head for the Olympic Games in Germany later that year. And, inspired by this global contest, Charlie and John soon embark on their own Moon Olympics, beginning with some throwing sports – hurling packaging and other unwanted items as far as they can.

"Tony, I'm going out for the Olympics," announces Charlie.

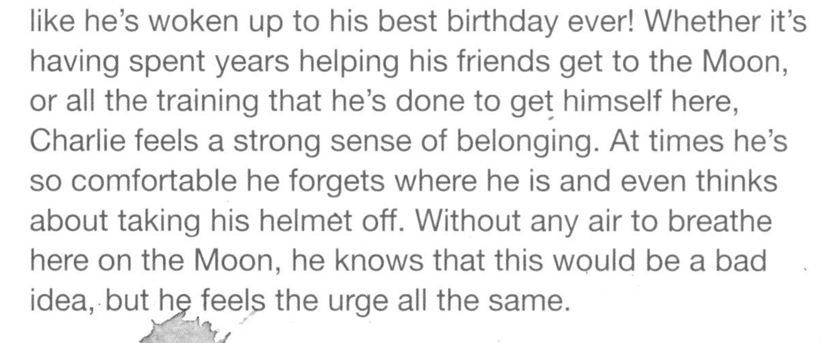

"I just slung that little carry bar about 200 metres, it looked like." He picks up another item and throws it as hard as he can. "There goes the other one," he reports. "I'm a real winner on the hammer throw. Look at that beauty go!"

"Outstanding, Charlie," replies Tony. "I'm sure you'll hold the record now."
"I doubt that," replies Charlie, remembering all the stuff his friends who've been on the Moon before have thrown in the lower lunar gravity.

While Charlie's been practising for the Olympics, John's unloading experiments from the base of the spacecraft, occasionally dropping to his knees to pick things up before springing back to his feet. It's a difficult manoeuvre to accomplish without toppling forwards, but John has already mastered it.

Charlie glances over at John. "You are black from the knees down already," he says.
"I know, I've been on my knees twice to get things," replies John. "No way to avoid it. That's why I'm glad the pressure suit bends."

The space suits that he and John are wearing, like those of the astronauts who've been here before, are miracles of engineering. Often referred to as wearable spacecraft, they carry everything required to keep a person alive beyond Earth – air to breathe, water to drink and temperature regulation to keep them at their peak. But to do this, the air pressure inside the suits makes wearing them feel like working against a giant balloon. And bending their shoulders, elbows, knees and ankles is only possible thanks to a clever concertina of rubber and wires built into each joint of the suit. The design was inspired by watching how a tomato worm bends its body as it crawls along a leaf. These marvellous suits, which have slowly been improved in the years since humans have been coming here, allow John and Charlie to move quite easily.

With the flag up, Charlie decides to take a few tourist photos. "Hey, John, this is perfect, with the LEM and the rover and you and Stone Mountain. And the old flag," he announces. "Come on out here and give me a salute. Big Navy salute."

John steps into view and flexes his right shoulder joint to adjust the restraining cables so that he can salute. "Look at this," he calls.

Tony is watching on the TV back on Earth. "That's a pretty outstanding picture here, I tell you," he reports.

"Come on, a little bit closer," instructs Charlie. "OK, here we go. A big one."
John responds by bending his knees slightly and launching himself off the ground as he salutes. In lower gravity than he's used to on Earth, John's efforts keep him off the ground for almost one and a half seconds. It's like he's levitating.

Tony chuckles in delight at the sight on his TV monitor.

"Off the ground. Once more," requests Charlie, keen to make sure he gets a good shot. "There we go," he says, snapping another photo of John in the air. Charlie takes the camera off the clip on his chest and hands it to John to take some shots of him in return.

"I'd like to see an Air Force salute, Charlie," requests John, "but I don't think they salute in the Air Force," he jokes as a former (rival) Navy pilot.
"Yes, sir, we do," replies Charlie, keen to correct him. Charlie is an accomplished Air Force pilot who's often flown fast jets to the edge of space.
John laughs at how easy it is to wind up his friend.

"And fly high and straight and land soft," Charlie continues, sticking up for his Air Force pals.
"OK, Charlie, say when," requests John, ready with the camera.
"Here we go," announces Charlie doing his very best salute for the photo.
John snaps a slightly wonky picture at a jaunty angle.
"Do it again?" he asks.
"One for you. OK, wait a minute, one more," replies Charlie, saluting again.
"OK," says John, happier with his second and third slightly less wonky photographs.

The pair spend the next couple of hours laying out experiments and loading up the rover for their first short trip – a two kilometre drive westwards to visit a number of small craters called Flag, Plum and Spook.
"Man, this is the only way to go, riding this rover," announces Charlie.
"Right. Only way," agrees Tony.
"You can hear the motors going, Tony," says Charlie, feeling the vibrations from the wheels travelling through the vehicle, up through the seats and into his suit.

The ground in front of them looks quite flat at a glance, trailing off far ahead towards a couple of hills on the distant horizon. The Sun is behind them, which would make for perfect driving conditions on Earth. But here on the Moon, this washes out the terrain ahead and makes it hard to spot obstacles like small craters and boulders hiding in the shadows they're casting.

"We're still in this boulder field," reports Charlie looking around them. The surrounding rocks are all quite angular blocks of breccia, the type that Neil and Buzz found, made up of lots of fragments of other rocks.
"Biggest one I see is about, oh, in the 12 o'clock position of the rover," notes Charlie, meaning it's straight ahead of them. "And it's about a metre across," he estimates.

Blinded somewhat by the bright sunlight behind them, John drives on cautiously at around five kilometres per hour. It's a bouncy ride and the back end of the rover sometimes slides sideways. Both astronauts are pleased to be wearing seat belts.

"How's it driving, John?" asks Charlie. "Pretty easy?"

"Darn good," replies John.

Charlie is playing tourist as John drives, snapping photos as they go and checking the map. It's a little cramped riding together and Charlie starts to bump John's driving arm, causing him to briefly lose control.

"Charlie, you hit my arm," John cries.

Charlie doesn't seem to notice as he tries to answer some questions from Tony about the rocks, and doesn't hear John.
He does it a second time, annoying John again.

"Quit hitting my arm!" John shouts.
Charlie is still talking to Tony about the rocks.
"I haven't seen any that I'm convinced is not a breccia," he says, continuing to ignore John's protest.

John's now struggling with Charlie and the sunlight.
"Driving down-Sun in zero phase is murder," he grumbles.
"It is, isn't it," sympathises Charlie.
"It's really bad," replies John, as he hits another unseen rock and the rover takes off.
"You're making great time, though," says Charlie encouragingly.

"Tony, we're parking right on the rim of Plum," reports John, pulling to a halt.
"OK," replies Tony.

While John and Charlie walk over to start photographing and sampling around the edge of Plum, the backroom science team spots an interesting rock in the foreground. It appears to have a huge, pale, crystal face staring out at them, meaning that it might be the same as Dave's Genesis Rock. Forty minutes later, as John and Charlie head back, Tony asks Charlie if he'd pick it up for them. It's quite large – larger than anything Charlie would normally attempt to pick up.

"This one right here?" asks Charlie pointing at it.
"That's it," says Tony.
"That one right here?" Charlie checks again, now pointing with this scooping tool. He can't quite believe it.
"That's it," repeats Tony. "You got it, right there."
"OK, that's a..." begins Charlie.
"…that's a football-size rock," finishes John.
"It's a 'Great Scott' size," says Charlie, referring to the nine-kilogram rock that Dave picked up near Hadley Rille. But this one is bigger, almost three kilograms bigger, the weight of a couple of bowling balls on Earth.

"Are you sure you want a rock that big, Houston?" asks John.
Charlie is leaning on his scoop, beside the rock, while he waits for an answer.
"Yeah, let's go ahead and get it," confirms Tony.
"OK," says Charlie, bracing himself for the effort.

Too big for the scoop, Charlie drops to his knees and rolls the boulder over towards his right leg.
"It's got some big clasts in it, John," Charlie notes, spotting fragments of other rocks and crystals within it.
"It sure has," agrees John, taking a glance.

Still unable to get his fingers underneath the rock, Charlie digs his glove tips into its side and tries to walk his fingers around it, rolling the rock on to his thigh. It falls off.

"Argh!" he calls out in frustration, leaning forward further against the pressure of his suit to get his hand around the rock enough to press it into his leg. As he stands, the rock rises with him, pinched between his limbs.
"If I fall into Plum Crater getting this rock, Muehlberger has had it," he jokes, referring to their geology teacher Bill Muehlberger. They name the rock "Big Muley" after Bill. It will be the largest rock sample ever collected on the Moon. The latest analysis estimates its age at 3,970 million years.

"OK, I've got it!" cries Charlie triumphantly. "That's 20 pounds of rock!"
"You want to put it in here, Charlie?" asks John, offering up a sample bag. "I'd just as soon you didn't. Look at the size of that moose!"
"I know it," agrees Charlie. "Oh, Tony! It's got some beautiful crystals in it though. That was a good guess."
Charlie reaches out to try and get it into the sample bag.
"OK, put it in there, John."
"Put it in where?" says John, changing his mind. "I don't think it'll fit."
"It ain't gonna fit," repeats Charlie.
"Put it under your seat," offers John.

Another 40 minutes later, on their way back to the spacecraft with their first stash of rocks, Charlie and John prepare to shoot a film that will become one of the most famous movies ever made on the Moon.
The engineers who created the rover have still not seen how it drives at speed across the hummocky lunar surface. They've only seen footage from on board the vehicle. But today Charlie will film what they're calling *The Lunar Grand Prix*.

"Here's a flat place, sort of," says John, stopping to let Charlie off the rover with the movie camera. Charlie steps back a bit and starts rolling the camera as John

makes a close pass by him, heading off towards their spacecraft in the distance. Charlie pans the camera round, following John as he accelerates across the undulating ground, the wheels regularly lifting off.
"Man, you are really bouncing!" says Charlie.
"OK, that's 10 kilometres," announces John, relaying his speed.

Dust flies up behind him, arcing off the rear wheels into the sky in dramatic flurries that remind Charlie of a cockerel's tail feathers.
"He's got about two wheels on the ground," reports Charlie for Tony's benefit. "There's a big rooster tail out of all four wheels. And as he turns, he skids. The back end breaks loose just like on snow."
About 70 metres away from Charlie, John starts to make a turn.
"Come on back, John," calls Charlie.
John accelerates back towards Charlie, the rear wheels sliding out again as they slip in the deep pockets of dust that John's motoring through.
"OK, when he hits the craters and starts bouncing is when he gets his rooster tail. He makes sharp turns. Hey, that was a good stop. Those wheels just locked," continues Charlie, cutting the camera as John speeds past him again.

John drives another circuit for Charlie to record a few more minutes of footage.
"I have a lot of confidence in the stability of this contraption," John tells everyone, chuffed by his test run across the rough, rocky plain.

Back at the spaceship, John and Charlie clean themselves up and head inside. Although they've been careful to keep hydrated and topped up with energy during their time outside, using the drinking straw and fruit bar inside their helmets, Tony is concerned that they top up on a particular element called potassium, to keep their hearts healthy. To do this they've been instructed to drink plenty of orange juice, and John has had enough of it.

"I'm going to turn into a citrus product is what I'm gonna do," he tells Tony.

"Oh, well it's good for you John," replies Tony, urging them to drink up for their own good.
"Ever hear of acid stomach, Tony?"
"We'll give you a buffer when you get down," replies Tony, promising a tablet to reduce the acid when they get home.

Unaware he's still transmitting his voice to Earth, John continues to grumble. "I have the farts, again. I got them again, Charlie. I don't know what the hell gives them to me. I think it's acid stomach. I really do."
"It probably is," agrees Charlie.
"I mean, I haven't eaten this much citrus fruit in 20 years!" laughs John. "I like an occasional orange. Really do. But I'll be durned if I'm going to be buried in oranges."

John and Charlie's second drive on day two takes them south towards Stone Mountain. They'll travel over some of the roughest and most challenging terrain ever crossed on the Moon.

"OK, give me that first heading again, Charlie," says John as they board the rover.
"One-six-four," replies Charlie, giving John the compass heading he should follow to take them south. John pushes the T-handle controller forward and the vehicle sets off.
"Houston. We're underway," announces Charlie.
"You're only leaving two minutes late," reports Tony. "Outstanding!"
"You're kidding," says John in jest. "We must have forgot something, Charlie," he laughs.
"That's all I got to say..."

John picks out a route along a high ridge, which gives them spectacular views of Stone Mountain up ahead. His main job once again is to pick a course that avoids the larger boulders scattered around them. Their path begins to drop downslope, increasing their speed a little and adding to the challenge of avoiding the larger obstacles. At one point, the rear wheels slide out from behind them.

"Yeow! Whooo! Man, that was a great big skid," calls Charlie. "We're doing 10 clicks, Tony."
"Outstanding!" replies Tony.

Undaunted by the skid, John points the rover south and continues winding his way towards Stone Mountain. The rocky debris around them starts to increase. Thankfully the sunlight is coming in to the side of them, making it much easier to spot the ones to avoid.

The slope rises again, and the size of the blocks around them grows to more than a metre and a half.
"That's gonna be a steep slope up there, John," says Charlie.
"I believe it is, Charlie," replies John, swerving abruptly to avoid another obstacle. As he does, the front wheels spray Charlie with dust.
"Aw, shoot, man!" exclaims John.
"Golly. Covered me with dust on that one," remarks Charlie.
"Sorry Charlie," John apologises.

It's getting harder to pick their way through all the boulders. Impact upon impact has hurled rocks out in ray patterns around them – now covering at least half the ground in rubble.
"Boy, you just can't believe the blocks, Houston," observes John. "Got to get out of these, Charlie," he adds, looking for a route away from all the debris.
"I think you can hook a right here a little bit, John," suggests Charlie. "Looks pretty good."

John steers to the right to pick out a safer path. To make their passage harder, the plain is also littered with thousands of small craters. Many of them are quite old and worn down, allowing John to drive over them. But it makes the rover buck and kick as if it's trying to throw them off.

"Hey, that was super," shouts Charlie exhilarated by the ride. "That wheel just left the ground."

"This is the wildest ride I was ever on," agrees John.
"I love it," cries Charlie. "It's great! Eight clicks, Tony. We got up to 12 there, once."
"Sounds like you're really making money there," Tony replies.

The route steepens as they push on up Stone Mountain to their highest point.
"Man, we are really going up a hill, I'll tell you," says Charlie. "This is going to be spectacular!"
John accelerates again to keep them climbing.
The slope is so steep that they begin to feel as if they're going to fall out the back.
"Look at this slope. Look at what we have been coming up. Man."
John finds a relatively flat spot and parks the rover up.
"OK. We're parked, Tony," reports Charlie.

Now over a kilometre south of their landing site, and more than 230 metres above it, this could be the most spectacular view any astronaut has ever seen on the Moon.
"Tony, you just can't believe this!" marvels Charlie. "You just can't believe this view! You can see the lunar module. Wow! What a place! What a view, isn't it, John?"
"It's absolutely unreal!" replies John, lost for words.
"We've really come up here, Tony. It's just spectacular," continues Charlie. "Gosh, I have never seen...All I can say is 'spectacular', and I know y'all are sick of that word, but my vocabulary is so limited."
"We're darn near speechless down here..." replies Tony, staring at the pictures from the TV camera that they're now looking at, back on Earth.

John and Charlie busy themselves taking photographs, making measurements and collecting samples. Working up here feels so exhilarating. Charlie can't quite believe what's just happened. Not only has he made it to the Moon, but he's now ridden a car up a mountain there too!
"Boy, this is so neat," he calls out "Ha! Man, am I having a good time."

One of Charlie's jobs up here is to measure how soft the ground is by attempting to push a rod about a metre long, known as a penetrometer, into the dirt. To carry out the experiment, Charlie must lean hard on the top of the rod. As he does so, the pole sinks into the ground further and faster than he's expecting, leaving him balancing on it, with his whole body at an angle. In an attempt to stand upright again, Charlie steps towards the instrument – but the soft ground won't support him and he ends up falling to his hands and knees.
"Argh! Rats!" he exclaims.
It's not the first time he's fallen over today and it won't be the last. Luckily he's becoming quite good at getting up again by using his arms to spring himself back upright from a press-up position; something he could never do on Earth.
"How'd you like that?" he calls out to Tony, aware he's been caught on camera.
"Beautiful manoeuvre there, Charlie," Tony compliments him. "What do you do for an encore?"

"I'll tell you one thing, we're sure up in the air," says John, using an Earth expression for being high up even though there's no air here to be up in!
"Yep," agrees Charlie, still gasping at the view.
Their stop here on Stone Mountain is the highest point anyone will ever reach on the Moon, and both of them literally feel on top of the world.

After 40 minutes working up here, they set off for the drive down – this time feeling as if they're going to fall out forwards as John points them straight back down the steep slope.

Just for fun, John lets the rover run away with itself down the side of the mountain for a few metres.
"Ya-ho-ho-ho-ho," he shrieks in excitement. "Look at this baby. I'm really getting confidence in it now," he brags. "It's really humming like a kitten."
"Oh, this machine is super," cheers Charlie.
"Probably a good idea you couldn't see how steep it was going up," Tony suggests.
"Darn right it was," agrees John, as the rover continues to dash away downhill under its own steam. "OK. I've got the power off and we're making 10 kilometres an hour. Just falling down our own tracks," he boasts.

To reach the next stop, they must climb again up a ridge to the west towards a crater called Wreck. To try and stay in control, John takes the slope by steering at an angle across it. But he still needs to stay on top of the steering to avoid boulders.

"Uh-oh!" he cries as he tries to avoid another one, only to find the rover's speed has rendered his steering useless. It suddenly feels more like he's driving on ice than through moon dust. Charlie is getting thrown all over the place during their descent and at one point – while he's trying to manage the maps, the camera and the communications antenna – his hand hits the console and knocks some of the switches, killing power to the rear wheels. Neither of them notices the problem until a few minutes later, when John realises that the rover has lost power.

"Have you got full throttle on?" asks Charlie, feeling the lack of pull.
"I got full throttle," replies John, also concerned by the lack of power.
"Boy, we're hardly moving," reports Charlie.
"OK, you want to read some amps?" asks Tony, offering to troubleshoot for them.
"OK, what it is, is we've lost the rear-wheel drive," explains John.
"OK, understand," says Tony.
"Not reading any amps on the rear wheel," observes John.
"OK, we copy that," confirms Tony.

"John, why don't we check it?" suggests Charlie. "It just might be a steep slope."
"No, Charlie. The ammeter was reading zero!" replies John. "If the slowdown had been due to the slope, they would expect the meter to show a large current," he explains.
"I know. Could be a broken meter," offers Charlie.
John is worried that he's driven it too hard and maybe broken a cable on some rocks. The pair limp on to their next stop, anxious that this could be their final drive.

While they get to work exploring, Tony rounds up some ideas for what could have gone wrong.

"OK, John, we'd like you to try the PWM 1 on the Left Rear and Right Rear," he suggests, pointing them to a switch which might restore power to the rear wheels. John reaches over and flips it. The rover's full power returns instantly.

"Oh, that's the problem!" says John sheepishly, realising what must have happened. "Somehow this guarded switch got moved to...Oh, isn't that amazing."
"Amazing," says Charlie, relieved they won't be walking home.

The pair make one last stop on the way back to the spacecraft, exhausted and covered in dirt. Charlie has fallen over at least six times today. But he doesn't mind a bit. He and John have had the best day of their lives. They've been outside here on the Moon for almost seven and a half hours straight, and that night they will sleep longer and deeper than any other astronauts have on another world – not stirring for over seven hours.

On their final day on the Moon, John and Charlie drive in the opposite direction towards Smoky Mountain and North Ray, in search of even older rocks. By the time they're done, they've driven over 26 kilometres across the Descartes Highlands, setting a new Moon speed record of 17 kilometres per hour.

Back near the spacecraft, and preparing to head home, there's something Charlie has been longing to do. He takes a small photograph out of one of his pockets and drops it gently on to the Moon. The photo is of him and his family – his wife Dottie in a blue dress, seven-year-old Charles in a shirt and tie and five-year-old Tom in a red T-shirt. Before he left Earth, he wrote on the back: "This is the family of Charlie Duke from planet Earth, who landed on the Moon on the 20th of April 1972." They have all signed it and added their thumbprints. Charlie steps back and snaps three photos of it. The last one is the best, capturing the surreal sight of a frozen moment in time, as these smiling faces from Earth stare out at us silently from the lifeless Moon.

Like Dave and Jim before them, they will drive their rover back out again one last time to its final resting spot looking back at the LEM. But before they set off, John wants to try one last Olympic Moon event. Standing beside the rover and grabbing the back of his seat to steady himself, he starts to jump on the spot, getting higher and higher with each leap. Finally he lets go of the rover for his last jump, launching himself about 70 centimetres off the ground.

"For a 380-pound guy, that's pretty good," praises Tony.

Not wanting to be outdone, Charlie makes his own giant leap, beating John with a height of around 80 centimetres. But instead of landing safely like John, Charlie's backpack pulls him backwards and, although he just manages to land on his feet, he can't stop himself from toppling back, crashing on to his life support system.
"Charlie!" exclaims John, worried he's broken his oxygen supply.
"That ain't any fun, is it?" says Charlie, feeling foolish, and somewhat anxious that he's now about to die.
"That ain't very smart," says John, scolding him.
"That ain't very smart," repeats Charlie, struggling to get up. "I'm sorry about that."

Charlie's covered in dust again. John gets the brush out to clean him off.
"Right! Now we do have some work to do," he announces, reaching over to pull Charlie up.

With Charlie rescued and cleaned up a bit, John turns his attention back to their checklist.
"OK. I want to park the rover."
"Charlie, we'd like you to dust that panel and the top of the console," Tony requests.
"All right, sir. Just a moment," replies Charlie, grabbing his brush.
"Why do you want to do that, Houston?" asks John.
"We want to keep the temperature of the panel down," Tony replies.
"In case anybody comes back?" asks John.
"I guess so. Keep it nice for the next guy," chuckles Tony.
"OK," laughs John.

Mission Control aren't expecting anyone else to visit the rover up here on the Moon, but by keeping it as clean as possible, it should avoid any dark dirt absorbing more sunlight and overheating the rover's electronics. They're hoping it will survive another few Earth-weeks here, for the rest of the long lunar day, allowing them to pan the camera around and keep watch over the Descartes Highlands after John and Charlie have left.

"You know, we sure hope you guys have enjoyed watching this as much as we've enjoyed doing it," declares John.

"We've sure enjoyed watching, I can tell you," says Tony.

The Taurus-Littrow Valley
Monday December 12th 1972

On the surface of the moon

Gene Cernan CDR
(Commander)
Jack Schmitt LMP
(Lunar Module Pilot)

Voice from earth

Bob Parker (Capsule Communicator)

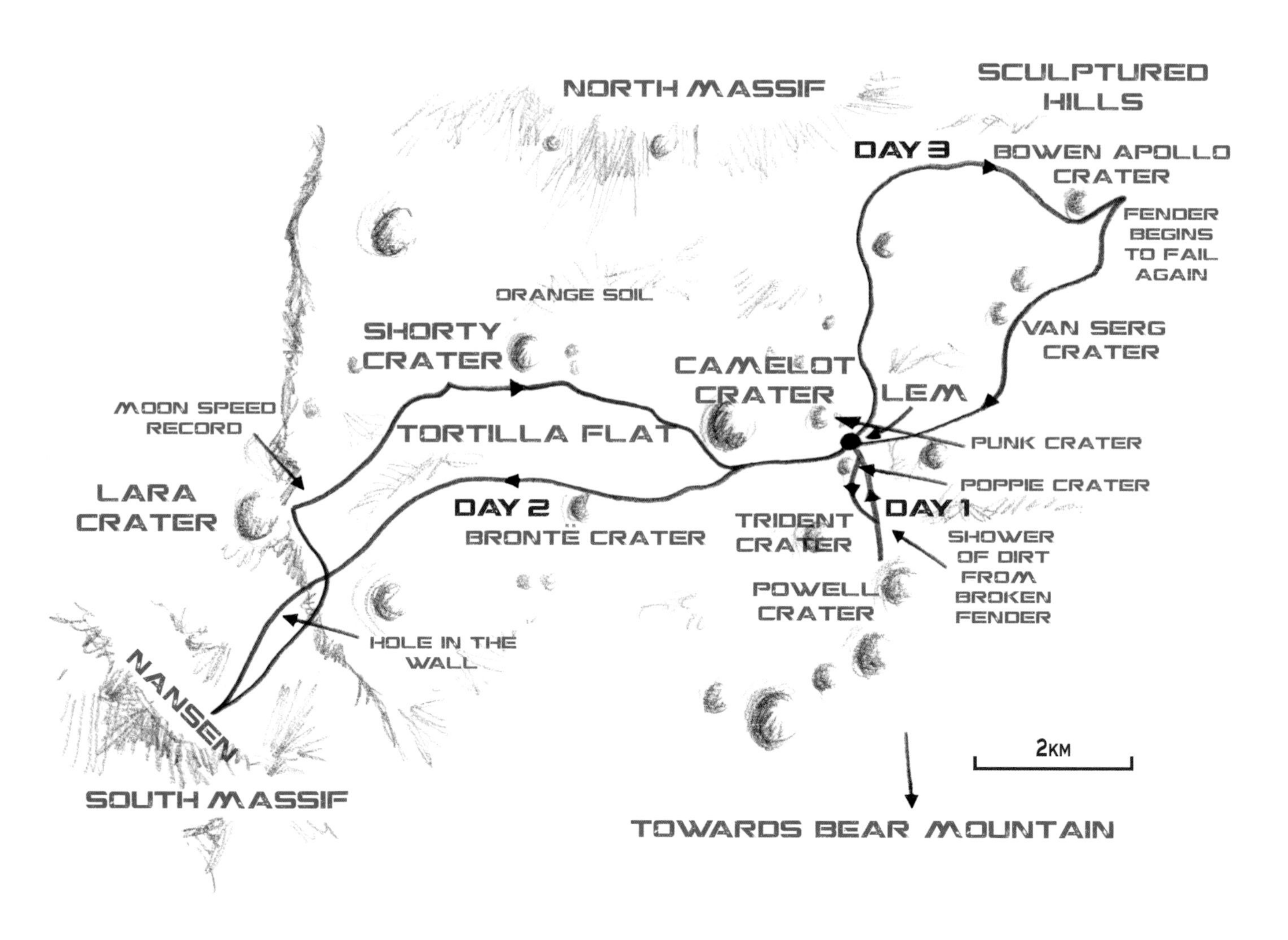

Apollo 17 landing site map

"Jack, I'm out here," calls Gene. He takes his first few steps on the Moon, dancing joyfully out of the spacecraft's shadow. "Oh, my golly! Unbelievable! Unbelievable – but is it bright in the Sun."

Gene and Jack have landed in a valley deeper than the Grand Canyon on Earth, called Taurus-Littrow. Brightly lit mountains rise all around them into the blackest of black velvet skies. One of the first things that strikes Gene is just how silent it is. All he can hear inside his helmet is the sound of his own breathing. He holds his next breath, and hears absolutely nothing.

He breathes again, turning back to face the spaceship. "The LEM looks beautiful," he declares. Gene is wondering precisely where they've landed. "Let me see exactly where we are," he says. "I think I may be just in front of Punk." Punk is the name Gene has given to one of the nearby craters he was aiming for when they were coming in to land. It's also his nickname for his nine-year-old daughter Tracy.

Gene glances around the valley again towards the North Massif. "Oh, do we have boulder tracks coming down," he announces, spying the marks left by a nearby rockfall. "A couple of large boulders... Looks like where we can get to them; there's a couple I know we can get to."

He turns to the east, facing the Sun. Sculptured Hills to the north and Bear Mountain to the south stare down blankly as they have for almost four billion years.
He tries to describe them. "The Sculptured Hills are like the wrinkled skin of an old, old, 100-year-old man," he begins. "That is probably the best way I could put it. Very, very hummocky, but smoothly pockmarked."

"OK. We copy that, Gene," says a man called Bob Parker, who's sitting back on Earth listening in. Bob's an astronomer and has never flown into space. But he hopes to one day. "Have you got an LMP with you yet?" he asks, referring to Jack – Gene's Lunar Module Pilot.

"Well, here come his feet," says Gene looking up at the hatch as Jack clambers eagerly out. "Jack, you're looking good," adds Gene, before setting off again on a walk around the spacecraft.
He's still trying to pinpoint exactly where they've touched down.
"I think this is Poppie," he notes, referring to a crater he's named after the nickname his daughter uses for her grandpa.

Jack has made it on to the spacecraft's porch, just outside the hatch, and he's already looking around. "Hey, who's been tracking up my lunar surface?" he cries, grumbling at how many footprints Gene's already made. Jack is a geologist, the first professional scientist to reach the Moon, and he's keen to get a first look at everything in this ancient valley before it's disturbed.

"Hey, Bob, how big is Poppie supposed to be?" asks Gene.
"It looks on the map like it's about 75 metres in diameter," replies Bob.
"OK, I tell you where I think I landed...Oh, about 100 metres from Poppie at 10 o'clock," concludes Gene.
"You think that's Poppie, huh?" Jack asks.
"I think so. I think..." Gene replies, sounding unconvinced.
"That's an awful big hole," continues Jack, sounding even more sceptical.

"Well, I know. I got to look around a little more," acknowledges Gene. "God, it's beautiful out here."

Jack jumps back up to the first rung of the ladder to reach the lanyard they will pull to release their rover.
"You're pretty agile there, twinkletoes," laughs Gene.
"You bet your life I am," Jack boasts.

The two of them work together to tug their car out on to the Moon. All the pulling and straining makes Jack a little warm. Bob suggests he turn up his suit's cooling system. Jack turns a dial and his backpack starts to pump more cold water through tiny tubes running close to his skin, to carry the heat away.
"How's my cooling look now, Bob?" he asks.
"It's come down quite a bit," replies Bob. "Looks much better. We didn't want you to sweat."
"Well, I'm just a hot geologist," jokes Jack, "that's all!"

Gene begins to test out the rover to make sure the hand controller works. "She goes forward and she goes reverse," he says, running through his checks.

Before loading the vehicle, Gene takes it for a spin around the spacecraft. "OK. Here we go. There's life in this here baby," he cries in delight. "Beautiful."
Jack snaps a series of photos as Gene drives back.
"Come towards me, baby!" cries Jack.
"Oh, boy," shouts Gene, exhilarated by the feeling of driving on the Moon.

Gene pulls up again beside Jack, and the two of them start laying out the experiments, before they turn their attention to putting the flag up. It's a flag that's hung in the room where Bob's sitting back on Earth, since Neil and Buzz made the first journey here.

"This has got to be one of the most proud moments of my life. I guarantee you," says Gene, posing for a photo next to it.
Jack snaps a few shots of Gene and hands the camera to him.
"Well, I want to get something here," says Gene.
"What's that?" asks Jack.
"I want to get the Earth," Gene replies.

The Valley of Taurus-Littrow is further east than the other landing sites, meaning that the Earth is hanging lower in the sky than the others have seen it – just over a mountain to the south that they call the South Massif. But it's hard to photograph without getting the camera low down and looking up.

Gene starts to bend his knees and swing the camera below his waist, tilting it up blindly. His first snap is filled with flag. He drops even lower and backs off, now almost on his knees, and tries again. It's a perfect framing, with Jack leaning in slightly and the flagpole pointing the way to Earth 400,000 kilometres above their heads. They trade places, but Jack can't get as low. He tries a couple of times. Almost on his knees, he just manages to get Gene, the flag and the Earth in, but it's not as artful as Gene's picture.

With time ticking on, the two of them get back to work setting up experiments. There's a lot to unpack from the spacecraft and, while moving equipment around, Gene catches a hammer in his shin pocket on one of the rover's rear mud guards. It tears the back half off.

"Oh, you won't believe it,"Gene announces, feeling the tug but unable to stop in time. He looks down to clock the damage. "No! There goes a fender."
"Oh, shoot!" replies Jack, aware of the consequences.

The fenders, as they call them, are there to stop the rover throwing moon dust over them as they drive. And with one now partially missing, Gene and Jack stand to get a whole lot dirtier. This matters because the dust is so sharp and jagged that there will be more chance of parts of their suits wearing out faster. In addition, wherever the relatively dark moon dust lands, it absorbs more heat from the Sun, causing equipment to get too hot. Both men feel they already spend too much time constantly dusting off equipment and themselves. With less protection, that task could now take even longer.

"I hate to say it, but I'm going to have to try to get that fender back on," announces Gene, feeling bad about his mishap.

"Jack, is the tape under my seat, do you remember?" he asks, hoping that a few strips of a strong sticky tape, called duct tape, might stick it back on.
"Yes," replies Jack, not really paying much attention to Gene's problem.
Gene retrieves the sticky tape and starts work on the broken fender.
"Well, I've done this in training," he says unconvincingly. "I can't say I'm very adept at putting fenders back on. But I sure don't want to start without it."

Gene soon finds that the sticky tape doesn't like the dust and isn't as sticky as he was expecting. "Good old-fashioned American grey tape doesn't stick to lunar-dust-covered fenders," he reports.
"One more try." Gene drops the first piece of tape he'd tried and grabs the roll again to tear a second piece off. He struggles a little through his thick gloves, pressing it into place with one hand while smoothing it out with the other.

"Geno, how are you doing on that fender?" asks Bob.
"Bob, I am done!" replies Gene. "If that fender stays on...I'm going to take a picture of it because I'd like some sort of mending award. It's not too neat, but tape and lunar dust just don't hang in there together."

Gene grabs the repaired fender and gives it a tug to test it. "Well, let's hope. Keep your fingers crossed," he says, "and I'll be more careful around the fenders," he adds sheepishly.

The two of them carry on setting up experiments and attempt to drill a deep hole into the lunar surface to extract a core of rock. It takes a couple of hours and, as they go about their business, Gene's eye is constantly drawn back to Earth.

A third of the planet is in darkness as it turns above them on its axis. Having flown an earlier mission to orbit the Moon once before, Gene has seen the Earth as small and faraway as this more times than most astronauts. But he still finds it mesmerising; perhaps the most precious thing he will take away from all his experiences on the Moon.

"Oh, man. Hey, Jack, just stop," he calls.
"You owe yourself 30 seconds to look up over the South Massif and look at the Earth!"
"What? The Earth?" queries Jack.
"Just look up there," encourages Gene.
"Ah! You seen one Earth, you've seen them all," Jack replies dismissively.
Gene can't believe how indifferent Jack seems about seeing his home planet from here.
He tries again. "No you haven't, babe. When you begin to believe that..." his thought trails off as he gives up.

It's not that Jack isn't interested in the Earth.
As a geologist he's made it his life's work to study his planet – but he's already spent days looking at it from the spacecraft on the way here. In fact, after launch, Jack gave a running commentary for hours about every cloud and weather pattern he could see from the spacecraft. But now he's on the Moon, he feels duty bound to concentrate on the lunar surface and get the rover ready to explore.

Jack's a busy man – absorbed in his work.
So much so that he begins singing.
"I was strolling on the Moon one day..." he chimes out.
Gene, amused by Jack's rendition, joins in.
"...in the merry, merry month of May."
Jack changes the month to December to fit the actual date.
"No, May," corrects Gene.
"May," Jack repeats.
"May's the month this year," Gene reminds him.
"May. That's right," agrees Jack, continuing with the next verse.
"When much to my surprise, a pair of bonny eyes...

be-doop-doo-doo...” he trails off, forgetting the words.
“Sorry about that, guys, but today may be December,” says Bob correcting them both.

Fifteen minutes later, they’re ready to set off on their first drive. It will take them a short distance to the southeast towards a crater called Powell. Both buckle up, and with the navigation system pointing them in the right direction, Gene pushes the T-handle forwards and off they roll.

“Hey Bob, making 8 to 10 kilometres,” announces Gene, relaying their speed. “And I’m barely moving,” he adds, sounding unimpressed. The rover is not designed to go fast, but instead to carry two men and all their equipment as easily as possible around the landing site.

“We’re on the move, Bob,” Gene continues, beginning to weave around the bigger obstacles as the rover cruises gracefully through shallow craters, one wheel or two occasionally lifting off the ground. It feels like a slow-motion dance between the three of them – Gene, Jack and the rover – as they all bump along together, meeting and parting repeatedly.
Jack is loving the sporty ride. “Whee! Watch it,” he cries, as Gene swerves this way and that.
“Ho - ho - ho - hold it, hold it, hold it!”
“Got it, got it, got it...” shouts Gene, temporarily blinded by the bright sunlight he’s now driving into. “Boy, I tell you; I’ve got to get out east,” he calls, trying to manoeuvre on to a better heading.
“Stand by.”

“OK, the fenders are still on, thank goodness,” reports Gene.
“Beautiful. We’ll give you the ‘Taper of the Year’ award,” replies Bob mockingly.
“Boy, you’re going to have to give me the ‘Duster of the Year’ award after this,” jokes Gene.

Despite the rover’s navigation system and the map that Jack’s using to follow their progress, it still proves hard to identify the specific crater they’re trying to reach.
In the end they decide they’re close enough and park up to collect some samples. They’ve come about 1.2 kilometres, but can still see the spacecraft behind them when they look back. It looks tiny, set against the immense mountains beyond.
“Hey! Look at the *Challenger* down there,” says Gene. “Makes you get a feel for how big this valley really is.”

The two of them get to work chipping off pieces of rock from the boulders that are strewn around them. With the repairs to the fender, and other difficulties they had with some experiments and rock core samples, they’re a little bit behind.
“...driving in 10 minutes, please,” interrupts Bob.
“Nag, nag, nag,” replies Jack, frustrated they don’t have more time.
They set off again, heading north back towards the spacecraft, when suddenly Jack is aware that he’s getting covered in dust.
“I think you have lost a fender,” he warns. “I keep getting rained on here.”
“Oh, no!” replies Gene, feeling bad again about breaking it.
“Look at our rooster tail,” cries Jack, spotting the arcs of dust the rover is hurling into the sky behind them. Without the fender, and with no air to stop it here on the Moon, the dust from the rear wheel isn’t just flying backwards – it’s raining down all over them and even landing ahead of them.
“Oh boy, that’s going to be terrible,” sighs Gene. “That is really going to be bad. Boy, I don’t like losing that fender.”

By the time they’ve got back to the landing site, they’re filthy, and so is the rover.
“Oh, boy, the thing that makes me sick is losing that fender,” groans Gene. “I can stand a lot of things, but I sure don’t like that. Oh, man, I tell you, it’s going to take us half a dozen Sundays to dust. Look at that fender; that’s terrible.”

Worried about managing these dust problems over the next couple of days, on much longer drives, the two of them start to think of solutions.
“Figure out something we can make a fender with?” Gene begins.

"How about one of the others that's not as critical?" Jack says, proposing they use one of the other fenders.
"Yeah, but I wouldn't ever take one of those off!" replies Gene.
Bob has been listening in. "OK," he says, "we'll take a look at it here while you're sleeping."

Before they can get back inside the spaceship, they need to clean each other off.
"It is going to be bad, but we want to get as much off as we can," says Gene, giving Jack a good brush down.
"It's taking some of it off," notes Jack, grabbing the brush to clean Gene off.
"OK?" Gene asks Jack, hoping he's clean enough.
"No. You're not OK," replies Jack. "You're awful dusty. But I don't know that I can do too much more."
"That looks pretty good," says Gene.
"Hit your boots real hard when you come up," suggests Jack.

Back inside the spacecraft, they shut the hatch and pump air into the cabin. By the time it's fully pressurised again and they can remove their suits, they've been wearing them for over seven hours.
"Oh, doesn't that feel good. Whoo!" says Gene, taking his gloves off.
"Ohh! You don't have a tub of hot water I can soak my hands in, do you?" he asks, knowing they don't.
Their fingertips are bloodied and bruised from the pressure inside their gloves. They lift their visors and unlock their helmets. The scent of the moon dust hits them.
"Smells like gunpowder, just like the boys said," says Jack.
"Oh, it does, doesn't it?" agrees Gene, sensing a kind of metallic smell that the dust is emitting now it's exposed to the air.

Jack's eager to pick up a few rocks, so he can get a closer look at them without his helmet on. But to his annoyance, the dust is irritating his nose and he's starting to sound as if he has a cold. He's the only astronaut so far to show an allergic reaction to the moon dust.

It's time for Bob to take a break back on Earth, and he hands over to Joe – the man who helped Dave and Jim on their flight to Hadley Rille.
"Sounds like you've got hay fever sensors, as far as that dust goes," he jokes to Jack.
"It's come on pretty fast just since I came back," Jack replies. "I think as soon as the cabin filters most of this out I'll be all right. But I didn't know I had lunar dust hay fever!"
"It's funny they don't check for that. Maybe that's the trouble with the cheap noses, Jack," kids Joe.
"Could be," says Jack. "I don't know why we couldn't have gone and smelled some dust in the LRL just to find out," he suggests, referring to the Lunar Receiving Lab where all the moon rocks are stored back on Earth.

Joe tries to cheer Jack up. "We're getting a request, many requests, for a weather report," he says. "We've been missing your weather reports and wonder what the weather is on the Moon right now."

Jack is already in his hammock, preparing to sleep. He glances out one of the top windows. The Sun is still shining brightly in the lunar morning.
"Well, the Moon's weather is clear and sunny," he reports. "It's only scattered clouds, and all of those seem to be attached to the Earth!"
"Except for a cloud of dust around the right rear wheel of the rover, we've noticed," Joe jokes.
"Yeah, but that dissipates in the morning warmth," replies Jack, hopeful that the engineers back on Earth will find a solution while he and Gene sleep.

After five hours of rest, their aches and pains of yesterday have passed. Back on Earth, John, who also had problems with the fenders on his own rover on the Descartes Highlands, has been working on a fix for them. It involves taking four plastic-coated maps and taping them together to create a single stiff sheet about 38 centimetres wide and 48 centimetres long.

"You can further strengthen it if you tape an 'X' of tape across both sides of it," John suggests.

"Then remove clamps from both the utility light units," he continues. These are movable spotlights inside the spacecraft. "Open the clamp jaws to max. And then tighten the mounting bracket that you've got on it so it will [not] be swinging around. You got that, Gene?"

"Yes, sir," replies Gene, grateful for John's carefully thought out plan.

John has even been practising how to attach this to the rover while wearing a space suit, and he's concerned it will be difficult.

"One thing about it, doing it in a suit, you have to push in with your leg and hold; and it's sort of a two-handed job," he explains. "It works OK in one G for one man. But I'm not sure it's not a two-man proposition in one-sixth gravity. Over."

"OK. We'll take a look at it, babe," replies Gene, appreciatively.

Gene runs back over the procedure with John one more time.

"OK. Call me the little old fender maker!" he grins, as he starts work on the replacement fender.

Gene and Jack get back into their space suits and prepare to go outside again to fit it. The repair job takes about five minutes. Gene steps back to admire their handy work.
"Too bad we don't have one more clamp..." he concludes, worried about how well attached it is.
"I think that'll stop the rooster tail," says Jack positively.
"I think that'll stop a lot of it, Houston," reports Gene.
"The maps are configured," says Jack.
"OK," says Bob. "That sounds like a good attempt, men. We'll hope it works."

Gene takes a quick spin around the landing site to check if it's working.
"Jack, how's the rooster tall look on that fender?" asks Bob.
"Looks like it's going backwards," reports Jack.
"I don't see anything coming up over the top," confirms Gene.
"Looks like a good fix," adds Jack, eager to get motoring.
"Beautiful!" replies Bob.

Today's drive will be the longest ever made on the Moon – taking them a dozen miles south towards the giant South Massif mountain. Their first location is an hour's drive away.

As they cruise south, Jack offers everyone a running commentary of the geology unfolding before them. He even refers to the specific numbers of rock samples he's studied from previous missions to paint as detailed a picture as he can.

"Ooh, and there's Camelot," cries Jack excitedly as he lays eyes on a crater he's been looking out for. Jack's spent hours examining the craters they'll visit today from photos taken in orbit, but seeing each for the first time, down here on the ground, is something else.

"That is a 600 metre crater!" cries Gene as he clocks Camelot too.
"OK. And it is very blocky..." continues Jack. He estimates about a third of the area is covered in large blocks, some up to four metres in size, all excavated from deep below the surface during the impact that created Camelot Crater. But there are other boulders further south that Jack is more interested in; giant rocks that have tumbled down from higher up the immense South Massif mountain.

Photographs of the area taken by Dave from orbit, during his flight to Hadley Rille, suggest there's a narrow passage they might be able to drive through to get them up to these fallen rocks on the mountain's lower slopes. This gateway is known as Hole-in-the-Wall.

"I'm going to work my way up to Hole-in-the-Wall and from there on up, right?" offers Gene.
"That's good," confirms Jack, consulting the map.
Gene noses the rover south towards the pass and the giant mountain beyond.
"Boy, is that getting big," he remarks as the South Massif rises up. "Whoo-ee! Hold on."
Gene bounces the rover through a few shallow craters.
"Whoooee!" calls out Jack.
"Oh, boy!" cries Gene as the rover drops abruptly into the next crater, carrying them with it.
"That really gives me a strange feeling," laughs Jack, his stomach feeling like it's rising into his chest.
"Gives me a strange feeling too," replies Gene. "Those are not intentional," he says, apologising for the bumps.
"I understand," acknowledges Jack.
"I'm not sure I've got enough guts to make them intentional," Gene admits, worried about doing further damage to the rover.

Both men are anxious about what's ahead.
"Man, everything's getting to look big the closer you get. Hole-in-the-Wall looks more promising, though, Bob," notes Gene.
"Yeah, I don't think that's going to be any problem," agrees Jack.
"...until we get up and look back," says Gene.
"Oh, man, what a trip this is going to be. Golly."

As their route to the mountain looms ahead, Gene and Jack get their first good look at what lies beyond.

"Hey, Bob, Hole-in-the-Wall seems to be right there," says Gene, swinging the rover left to enter it. "It's very rolling and relatively smooth," he continues, sounding relieved.

Gene pushes the T-handle forwards again as the rover's wheels bite into the dust to haul them further uphill.
"And is she working! Come on, baby," he cries, coaxing the little car to keep going. "It's quite a machine, I tell you! I think it would do a lot more than we'd let it. Bob. How long have we been driving?"
"Man, this has been a trip," shouts Jack, excited.
He can't believe how intrepid it all feels as they press on into the foothills, pushing the limits of how far they can safely walk back to the spacecraft should the rover fail them.
"Man, I tell you. You know, we're really up on top of this thing. Whoo!" says Gene.

"You guys have been driving 64 minutes," reports Bob. "We estimate you've got about a kilometre and a half to go. You're doing great."

As they roll on through the foothills, the South Massif rears up at them overbearingly. At 2300 metres above the height of the valley, it's an imposing presence and makes Jack and Gene feel very small indeed.

"That is a high mountain!" says Jack.
"Jimmeny Christmas!" laughs Gene. "Listen, if the Earth goes behind it, we're changing Station 2."
Both men begin to laugh at the thought of Earth disappearing behind a mountain and blocking their communications to Bob.

Gene pulls up as they approach the boulders that have tumbled down the side of South Massif. The two of them unbuckle their seat belts and get to work.

"Hey, thank you for that fix on the fender, by the way, because I'd hate to see what it would look like without it," says Gene gratefully.
"OK," replies Bob.

Gene's gaze turns to the terrain around them.
"Man, there's some boulder rolling rocks here, Jack."

The pair spend most of the next hour meticulously taking photographs and collecting rocks, including a small white fragment they break off a grey boulder. This will later be found to be four and a half billion years old – one of the oldest rocks ever collected on the Moon.

"We ought to start moving out of here," announces Gene after about 50 minutes.
"Yeah, let's go," replies Jack.

Driving back down the escarpment, or scarp, Gene's thirst for speed kicks in and he pushes the rover a little too fast for Jack's comfort.
"Keep your speed down," pleads Jack, "because if you have to turn, it doesn't like it on a downhill slope."
This was how Dave spun the first rover here on the Moon, and Jack isn't keen to repeat that stunt!

A few seconds later, they clear the slope.
"We're off the scarp," calls Jack, sounding relieved.

"What was it, 17½ or 18 clicks we hit coming down the scarp, Jack?" Gene asks cheekily, aware that John only managed a top speed of 17 kmph on the Descartes Highlands. As a big fan of motorsport, and the last man to drive on the Moon for some time to come, Gene's keen to clinch the title of fastest driver in the world – this world.

"I don't…" begins Jack, bursting into laughter at Gene's bravado, and keen not to encourage any more of his speed record attempts.

Jack's desperate to get to another crater called Shorty. He's eagerly scanning the landscape ahead of them in the hope of spotting it.

"Where are you, Shorty?" he calls.

Then a few minutes later he asks, "See Shorty out there yet?"
"Hold it, babe. We got to do a little detouring," replies Gene, negotiating the rover around a few obstacles. "I'll just get down this slope. I see Shorty though, do you?"
"Wait a minute, is that it?" cries Jack. "Is that it out there straight ahead? Something's dark out there. I think that's it."

NASA

The reason Jack's so excited is that Shorty appears odd in the photographs taken from orbit. It's not like all the other impact craters. It's not very wide, but it is extremely deep, and some people think it might be an extinct volcano. No one has ever found an extinct volcano on the Moon. Could Shorty be the first?

No sooner has Gene pulled up and parked than Jack is off towards the edge of the crater, launching into his trademark running commentary.
"OK, Houston," he begins. "Shorty is clearly a darker-rimmed crater. The inner wall is quite blocky but the floor is hummocky, as we thought it was in the photographs. The central peak, or central mound, is very blocky and jagged."

Jack readies his camera to capture the view. "OK, I'm going to take a pan while I'm waiting for you," he calls.
"OK! OK!" replies Gene.

Jack can't contain his excitement as he approaches the crater's edge.
"Oh, hey!" he suddenly exclaims, questioning what he's seeing. "Wait a minute..."
"What?" Gene asks.
"There is orange soil!" he shouts.
"Well, don't move it until I see it," Gene calls back.
Jack is ecstatic. "It's all over! Orange!"
"Don't move it until I see it," repeats Gene, aware of the implications of what Jack has spotted.
"I stirred it up with my feet," continues Jack, kicking at it again to uncover more, just as Gene arrives.
"Hey, it is! I can see it from here!" Gene agrees.
"It's orange!" repeats Jack, still hardly believing what he's found.

Gene wonders if it's an illusion, caused by looking through their gold visors. "Wait a minute, let me put my visor up," he says, pausing to take a second look.
"It's still orange!"
"Sure it is! Crazy!" says Jack.
"Orange!" repeats Gene, still surprised.
"I've got to dig a trench, Houston," demands Jack. desperate to prove it's a volcano.

"Copy that," says Bob, also excited by the reaction of all the geologists watching them back on Earth. "I guess we'd better work fast."
"Hey, he's not going out of his wits," chuckles Gene.
"It really is."
"Is it the same colour as cheese?" asks Bob, joking that the Moon is made of cheese. He's still not entirely convinced Jack and Gene aren't pulling his leg. But they're not. And the orange soil might mean that the Moon is still hot inside, with volcanoes erupting on the surface more recently than geologists anticipated. Jack's discovery could overturn scientists' thinking about the Moon's history and formation.
It's a big moment.

But Gene and Jack are running out of oxygen and they can't stay out here much longer. They've got just half an hour to try to determine if they really are standing on the edge of an extinct lunar volcano! Working as fast as they can to photograph and collect the orange soil, they even manage to hammer a metal tube deep into the ground, pulling out a couple of rock cores which reveal what lies beneath it.*
"Even the core is red!" exclaims Gene as they pull it up.
"Be careful with that," pleads Jack as Gene carries it back to the rover.
Both men race to load the rover with all the samples they've collected, and head back to the spacecraft, aware their time for exploring here is running out.

* Under the microscope, back on Earth, Jack and the other geologists will see that the orange soil is in fact made of lots of tiny, glassy beads. And although it seems Shorty Crater is not volcanic, the orange glass <u>has</u> come from very deep down inside the Moon – maybe 500 kilometres down. They will be the only rocks ever collected from so far beneath the lunar surface and they provide a unique glimpse into the Moon that no other rock samples have given.

Gene wakes up to his last day on the Moon, and opens the shades on the top windows. Out there in front of him hangs his home planet.

"OK, just took a quick peek up there," he reports to Houston. "I can't really see too much of the North American continent. South America looks pretty good. And it might be my eyeballs rather than the clouds up there, but it looks like most of the clouds are up into the north-central part of the southeastern United States."
"I have a satellite picture here," replies a man called Gordon listening back on Earth, "and that's about the way it looks."

How about that, Gene thinks to himself, waking up here on the Moon and giving Earth a weather report! "Well, it's sunny and pleasant in the valley of Taurus-Littrow," he replies.

Today will mark their final drive across the Moon, as they cross the valley northwards to the North Massif. The fender repair is still holding out as they reach their furthest point, but only just.
"Our fender's beginning to fade," calls out Gene. "Uh-oh, the clip came off," he continues, realising the clamp holding their improvised fender has come loose. "We'll have to fix that before we start. The outside one's holding, but the inside one's not." A further repair keeps them going for the rest of the journey.

Back at the spacecraft a few hours later, having driven a record breaking 34.8 kilometres in the last three days, Gene undoes the clamp and pulls off their homemade fender to bring back to Earth as a souvenir. "Hey, congratulate José on that fender, will you?" he tells Bob, calling John by his nickname. "Because I think he just saved us an awful lot of problems. He and whoever else worked on it."

The truth is that hundreds of people worked on the rover. Sending people to the Moon, and bringing them safely home, has taken hundreds of thousands more. So many different people with different talents and knowledge and backgrounds and skills were needed; every one of them dedicated to the single task of sending humans to explore another world. It was only by working together and putting their differences aside that the adventures in this book could have happened.

Before the last two explorers leave the surface of the Moon, there's one last thing for the two of them to do together. On the legs of their spacecraft is a plaque, like the one that Neil and Buzz read from three years before. Gene reads out the words on it;

"Here Man completed his first exploration of the Moon, December 1972 AD. May the spirit of peace in which we came be reflected in the lives of all mankind."

Gene continues, "This is our commemoration that will be here until someone like us, until some of you who are out there, who are the promise of the future, come back to read it again and to further the exploration and the meaning of Apollo."
Listening to Gene's words are children from 70 different countries, who have gathered at Mission Control to mark these final moments of human activity on the Moon – where once we stood.

While Jack cleans off the inside of their spacecraft in preparation for lift off, Gene drives the rover away to film the launch from the remote control camera. He dismounts, kneels as best he can and, with a single finger, he silently scratches his daughter Tracy's initials into the lunar dust.

Gene jogs back and prepares to climb up the ladder for the last time, mulling over what he should say as he takes his last step off the Moon. He feels the presence of all the men and women who devoted their lives to getting him and his fellow astronauts here. Every one of them a giant upon whose shoulders he stands right now.

NASA

The camera on the rover is tilting skywards. "As you guys say farewell to the Moon, we're looking up to the Earth," says Bob, "down here where you guys are returning pretty soon."

Gene takes one last look at the Earth too, still unable to express how it makes him feel. He's saddened that so few people have seen this sight with their own eyes. If only everyone back there could feel what he feels. But he knows that's impossible right now. No one else is coming back here anytime soon.

"Bob, this is Gene," he says. "As I take Man's last step from the surface, back home for some time to come but we believe not too long into the future, I believe history will record that America's challenge of today has forged Man's destiny of tomorrow. And, as we leave the Moon at Taurus-Littrow, we leave as we came and, God willing, as we shall return, with peace and hope for all Mankind.

Godspeed the crew of Apollo 17."

THE GIFTS OF APOLLO

Central Pacific Ocean, Earth
Tuesday 19th December 1972
7:24pm

The last men to walk on the Moon land back on Earth in the Pacific Ocean with a huge splash a few days before Christmas 1972. On board with them is a roll of film that Jack used to snap a series of pictures of their home planet as they hurtled away from it twelve days earlier. Jack took several photos that day but image number 22725 is the best. It captures a whole face of our planet, perfectly lit by the Sun. Intricate spirals of brilliant white clouds gleam against the deep blues of the Atlantic and Indian Oceans.

The world appears to be upside down as we would think of it. The pearly white, ice-covered continent of Antarctica is at the top. Below it is the warm red and brown sun-baked expanse of Africa and right at the bottom, the brilliant blue Mediterranean Sea, lapping at the edge of Europe and the Middle East. When it's first printed in the photographic labs, a few days later, its beauty will take people's breath away. The *Blue Marble* picture, as they call it, brings a new appreciation for the care we need to take of our home planet.

An annual 'Earth Day', now the world's largest environmental movement, is created and the campaigning group Friends of the Earth is born. New laws to protect the environment and wildlife are passed. As one person wrote at the time, 'on the way to the Moon we'd discovered the Earth.' Today, action to reverse the damage we've inflicted on our home planet has spread around the world. And on the banners of striking schoolchildren are emblazoned their own drawings and paintings of Jack's 'Blue Marble' view of Earth. It helps to remind us how small and easily damaged our home really is.

Geological history teaches us that the Earth has become less habitable in the past, when the climate has changed rapidly. And now we are causing it to happen again. Since Jack first snapped his Blue Marble picture, humanity's hunger for more and more resources has destroyed 60% of Earth's wild animal populations. The loss of so many creatures isn't just a terrible shame – it matters because they're all part of the life support systems that keep Earth habitable for us all.

Reversing our impact on the climate and biodiversity is the greatest challenge that has ever faced human civilisation. But daunting as this feels, it's worth remembering the stories told in this book. For as Gene Cernan, the last man to walk on the Moon, used to say: "Don't ever count yourself out. You'll never know how good you are until you try. Dream the impossible and then go out and make it happen. I walked on the Moon. What can't you do?"

Wrapped up with the mementos of remembrance, inside the pouch that Neil and Buzz left on the Moon, is a tiny silicon disc, with goodwill messages inscribed on it from leaders around the world. Their words are written in such small writing that you would need a microscope to read them. One message is from a man called Eric Williams – the then Prime Minister of a small, beautiful country called Trinidad and Tobago. It reads...

"It is our earnest hope for Mankind
that while we gain the Moon, we shall not lose the World."